10 MONTHS TO $1 MILLION:

Unlocking the Path to Financial Freedom, Transform Your Mindset, Amplify Your Wealth, and Achieve Extraordinary Success

Jeffrey Robinson T.

Copyright © 2024 [Jeffrey Robinson T.]

All rights reserved. No part of this book may be reproduced, distributed, or transmitted in any form or by any means, including photocopying, recording, or other electronic or mechanical methods, without the prior written permission of the publisher, except in the case of brief quotations embodied in critical reviews and certain other non-commercial uses permitted by copyright law.

Disclaimer:

The information provided in this book is for general informational purposes only and is not intended as financial, legal, or professional advice. The author and publisher make no representations or warranties regarding the completeness, accuracy, or reliability of the information contained herein. Readers are advised to consult with a qualified professional before making any financial decisions. The author and publisher shall not be liable for any losses or damages incurred as a result of the information provided in this book.

Table Of Contents

Introduction 5
Chapter 1: The Mindset Shift 8
    Understanding the Power of Your Mindset 8
    Breaking Free from Limiting Beliefs 11
    Cultivating the Mindset of a Millionaire 18
Chapter 2: Setting Your Goals 26
    Defining Your Vision For Success 26
    Setting SMART Goals for Financial Growth 33
    Creating a Strategic Plan of Action 38
Chapter 3: Taking Action 43
    Building Momentum with Consistent Action 43
    Overcoming Procrastination And Fear 45
    Leveraging Your Strengths and Resources 49
Chapter 4: Mastering Money Management 55
    Understanding The Flow Of Money 56
    Implementing Effective Budgeting Strategies 62
    Investing Wisely for Long-Term Growth 67
Chapter 5: Sales Mastery 74
    Unleashing Your Sales Potential 74
    Developing Persuasive Communication Skills 75
    Building and Nurturing Profitable Relationships 79
Chapter 6: Leveraging Technology and Innovation 85
    Harnessing the Power of Technology for Business Growth 85
    Embracing Innovation to Stay Ahead of the Curve 87
    Automating Processes for Efficiency and Scale 88
Chapter 7: Building a Strong Support System 91
    Surrounding Yourself with Positive Influences 91
Chapter 8: Overcoming Challenges and Adversity 94
    Embracing Failure as a Stepping Stone to Success 94
    Developing Resilience in the Face of Obstacles 97
    Turning Setbacks into Opportunities for Growth 101
Chapter 9: Scaling Your Success 104
    Scaling Your Business for Sustainable Growth 104
    Expanding Your Reach and Impact 107

Leaving a Lasting Legacy of Success... 111
Conclusion.. **114**

Introduction

In an era of rapid technological advancement, economic uncertainty, and unprecedented opportunity, the pursuit of financial freedom and extraordinary success has become more important or achievable than ever before. "10 Months to $1 Million: Unlocking the Path to Financial Freedom" is a comprehensive guide designed to provide you with the mindset, strategies, and tools necessary to transform your financial reality and achieve remarkable success in just ten months.

The foundation of this book lies in the deep belief that financial abundance is not a distant dream limited to the lucky few, but rather a tangible reality that can be achieved by anyone willing to adopt the right mindset and take decisive action. The Journey to a Million Dollars isn't just about accumulating wealth, it's about reshaping your relationship with money, harnessing the power of innovation, and leveraging strategic insights to achieve sustainable success in every area of your life.

Throughout the pages of this book, you will discover practical examples, proven tips, and actionable strategies drawn from the author's personal experience achieving $1 million in sales within a remarkably short time frame. By going against conventional wisdom and adopting a unique approach, the author shows how thinking differently and strategically can lead to extraordinary results.

Power of mindset

At the heart of this transformation lies the concept of mentality. The difference between those who achieve their dreams and those who don't often boils down to the way they think about money, success, and their own potential. This book delves into the mindset of millionaires, revealing how they think, act, and cultivate the habits that set them apart from the rest. By understanding and embracing these principles, you can join the 1% who achieve their financial dreams and break free from the constraints that hold others back.

Defining strategic goals and planning work

Achieving $1 million in 10 months requires a clear vision, strategic goal setting, and careful business planning. This book guides you through the process of defining your vision for success, setting SMART goals, and creating a strategic action plan tailored to your unique circumstances and aspirations. By breaking your journey down into manageable steps and maintaining constant focus on your goals, you can navigate the path to financial freedom with confidence and precision.

Harnessing technology and innovation

In today's digital age, technology and innovation are powerful enablers of business growth and efficiency. This book explores how you can leverage the latest technological advances and innovative practices to streamline operations, enhance productivity, and effectively scale your business. From automating processes and harnessing data analytics to embracing digital marketing and e-commerce, you'll learn how to harness the full potential of technology to accelerate your journey to $1 million.

Build a strong support system

No journey towards success is complete without a strong support system. Surrounding yourself with positive influences, seeking guidance and direction, and forming a network of like-minded peers are crucial elements in achieving your financial goals. This book emphasizes the importance of building a supportive environment that nurtures your growth, resilience, and overall well-being. By harnessing the power of community and collaboration, you can overcome challenges, stay motivated, and achieve extraordinary results.

Embrace continuous improvement and innovation

The path to a million dollars is not fixed; It requires continuous adaptation, improvement and innovation. This book encourages you to adopt a continuous improvement mindset, embrace emerging trends, and remain flexible in the face of evolving market dynamics. By fostering a culture of creativity, experimentation and lifelong learning, you can survive", "Ahead of the curve and take advantage of new opportunities for growth and success.

"10 Months to $1 Million: Unlocking the Path to Financial Freedom" is more than just a guide; It is a transformational plan for achieving financial success and personal fulfillment. By incorporating the principles, strategies, and ideas presented in this book, you can embark on a journey that not only redefines your financial reality, but also empowers you to live a life of purpose, abundance, and impact. The journey to a million dollars begins with one step - embrace the journey, believe in your potential, and open the path to financial freedom."

Chapter 1: The Mindset Shift

"[Positive mindset work] has allowed me to realize that I have more power in my life and my own choices."
— Riley T., former client

Have you ever felt stuck in a rut, unable to move forward to achieve your goals? You probably need to change your mindset. A mindset shift involves reframing the way we think about our lives and goals. It is an important tool for personal growth and development because it helps us identify areas of our lives that need improvement and the changes that will lead us to success. Let's take a look at how mental shifts can help us achieve our goals.

Understanding the Power of Your Mindset

Let's dive into the concept of mindset and how it can make a huge difference in our lives. Mindset is about the attitudes, beliefs, and perspectives that shape how we see and interpret the world around us. It is like a lens through which we see everything that happens to us.

Two basic mindsets have been widely studied: the fixed mindset and the growth mindset. Let's break it down.

First, we have a **fixed mindset**. Picture someone with a fixed mindset as someone who believes their qualities, abilities, and intelligence are set in stone. They believe that there is no room for change or improvement. Challenges? No, they try to avoid them like the plague because they fear failure and the potential embarrassment of revealing their limits. an effort? They consider it a waste of time because they believe that only natural talent determines success. When they encounter obstacles, they tend to give up quickly and feel threatened by the success of others. It is as if they are stuck in a rigid metal box.

On the other hand, we have a **growth mindset**, which is where the magic happens. Imagine someone with a growth mindset as someone who believes that qualities and abilities can be developed through dedication, effort, and learning. They are not afraid of challenges. They see it as opportunities for growth and learning. They realize that failure is just a natural part of the learning process, and they use setbacks as fuel to improve themselves. These people value effort, perseverance, and the idea that skills can be developed over time. In addition, they are inspired by the success of others and see this as a source of motivation and learning. It's as if they have an open and ever-expanding mental playground.

Now, here's the exciting part. The concept of mindset has gained a great deal of attention thanks to the pioneering work of psychologist Carol Dweck. Her research shows that people with a growth mindset are more likely to achieve their goals, overcome obstacles, and develop remarkable resilience. It's as if they have a secret weapon that drives them forward.

The best part is that the mindset is not fixed. It's not something you're born with and hold on to forever. No sir! You can develop and nurture your mindset over time. You have the ability to reach your full potential, take on challenges, and continually strive for personal and professional growth by cultivating a growth mindset.

So my friend, now that you understand the power of mindset and how it can shape your life, it's time to take action. I want to leave you with the following to push you toward adopting a growth mindset and unlocking your true potential.

Here's what I want you to do:

Reflection: Take a moment to reflect on your current mindset. Are there areas where you tend to have a fixed mindset? Are there challenges or opportunities that you have been avoiding because of fear? Awareness is the first step towards change.

Embrace Challenges: Start embracing challenges and setbacks as opportunities for growth. Instead of turning away from them, approach them with curiosity and a willingness to learn. Failure is not the end; It's just a starting point on your journey to success.

Cultivate a Growth Mindset: Nurture your mindset daily. Surround yourself with positive influences, read books or listen to podcasts that inspire growth, and participate in activities that expand your abilities. Train your mind to see potential and believe in your ability to develop new skills.

Perseverance and perseverance: Keep moving forward, even when things get tough. Remember, growth takes time and effort. Be patient with yourself, stay committed, and celebrate the small victories along the way. Your determination and perseverance will pay off in the long run.

Inspire and learn from others: Find inspiration from those who have achieved great things. Learn from their stories, strategies and experiences. Surround yourself with a community of like-minded individuals who support your growth journey.

Now, it's time to take these steps and get started on the path of growth and transformation. Embrace challenges, gain a growth mindset, and watch your life unfold with newfound possibilities.

Are you ready? I believe in you. Let's get out there and unleash the power of your growth mindset!

Breaking Free from Limiting Beliefs

What are limiting beliefs and how to break free from them?

There was a man who believed we would never be able to reach the moon.

On July 20, 1969, Neil Armstrong challenged that notion by becoming the first man ever to set foot on the moon.

There was a man who thought it was impossible to run a marathon in less than two hours.

On October 12, 2019, in Vienna, Eliud Kipchoge challenged this notion by breaking the two-hour marathon barrier with a time of 1:59:40.

There was a man who believed that a blind man could never summit a mountain.

On May 25, 2001, Eric Weinmayer challenged this belief by becoming the first blind person to reach the summit of Mount Everest.

There are many things in your life that may seem impossible.

The truth is it's not impossible, you just think it is.

"Whether you think you can or you think you can't, you're right." -Henry Ford

What Are Limiting Beliefs?
A limiting belief is an idea we have about ourselves or life that prevents us from achieving what we really want to achieve.

It starts with the limited idea that what we tell ourselves over and over again until we fully accept it and believe it to be true.

- "I'm terrible with money."
- "I could never be a business owner."
- "I'm not good at relationships."
- "No one loves me."
- "life is tough."
- "Every time I try to make a change, I fail."
- "Work is not meant to be fun."

All of the above are examples of limiting beliefs.

This is what is certain about them:

It's not true (we just think it is).

They started as an idea.

As we continue to affirm these ideas, they become beliefs.

We all have limiting beliefs that hold us back from our success.

As business mindset coach Nina Cook explains:

"Many limiting beliefs are created in our childhood. It is devastating that they become part of our identity. Taking the time to dismantle our limiting beliefs can free us to live a fuller, more fulfilling life, full of confidence and purpose."

Our limiting beliefs lie deep in our subconscious, thus preventing us from seeing or believing in possibility. Due to our minds' confirmation bias (the tendency to interpret new evidence as confirmation of our existing beliefs or theories), we tend to believe what we want to believe.

In essence, this is exactly why you think you are bad with money or why you think you are not worthy of true love, because you are unconsciously looking for reasons to confirm such beliefs.

So, if we really want to make positive change in our lives, we must first reset our pre-existing limiting beliefs – we need to break free from limiting beliefs.

As Dr. John Arden wrote in his book Rewire Your Brain:

"You can train yourself to change the way you think. By looking at possibilities rather than limitations on a regular basis, you will rewire your brain."

How to Break Free From Limiting Beliefs

"Eric Weinmayer's story is one of the most amazing stories I've ever heard.

When Eric was in ninth grade, he lost his ability to see. Naturally, he was struggling with this new reality of life, but that didn't stop him. He could have easily set limits on how far his life could go, but he didn't. Instead, he continued climbing the Seven Summits, the highest point on every continent on Earth.

"People fall into the trap of thinking of only one way to do things." -Eric Weinmayer

If he had listened to what others told him, "You're blind, you can't do this and that," or what he might have said to himself, "I can't see, so I can't do this and that." He will not overcome any of those adversities or mountains.

This is the liberating power of breaking free from limiting beliefs. It literally takes you on a journey of unlimited growth potential. It allows you to see what could be.

But the problem with our approach to breaking free from limiting beliefs is that we try to do it too quickly.

We go from telling ourselves "I was never good with money" to "I am good with money" and expect an immediate change in our behavior. But of course, we would be lying to ourselves, so no change would occur with such an approach.

The reality is this:

Change takes time. Changing behavioral patterns rooted in limiting beliefs takes longer. That's why you should take it one step at a time.

For example, here's how to reframe the limiting belief, "I was never good with money."

You start with "I've never been good with money, but I'm ready to see a change" and then you move on to "I'm working on improving my money management habits" and then "I'm open to reading books on money management and financial management." Learn from financial experts" and then "I am slowly getting better at managing my money and now I am excited to explore investment opportunities."

Do you see the difference?

When we move one domino at a time, day after day, we create sustainable change that will naturally move our thinking above the limiting beliefs that were preventing us from seeing that change for the first time.

Here are the four steps involved in this process:

- Recognize the limiting belief.
- They reject him.
- Reframe it into an empowering belief.
- Be willing to see change by taking it one step at a time.

When the story we tell ourselves is ingrained in our thinking, it's hard to notice it. That's why the first step in this process involves identifying the limiting belief. Any belief that begins with these words is considered a restricted belief:

"I'm not..."

"I can't..."

"I do not have..."

"It's always been this way..."

Once we become aware of those beliefs, we can reject them and then reformulate them into an empowering belief.

"I am..."

"I can..."

"I have..."

"There must be another way..."

As we explained earlier, we're taking it one step at a time.

"I won't be able to find remote work" becomes "I'm able to design a career path that will lead me to remote work."

"I'm not good at relationships" becomes "I can be a better partner and am working on becoming one."

"I'm not a confident person" becomes "I'm willing to become a confident person and I'm going to prove it to myself by taking action on what I don't feel confident about."

You need that shift in mindset. You have to be willing to see the possibilities. Otherwise, you will always find a reason why something doesn't happen or hasn't happened yet."

With that said, here's the biggest paradox:

You will not be able to overcome your limiting beliefs if you do not see real contradictory evidence in your behavior.

You wouldn't believe you could be good at money management if you didn't find evidence of your money management behavior. You will not believe that you can succeed in your ability to create a remote work life if you do not see evidence in your behavior that you are creating a remote work lifestyle.

think about it.

While you are the one who creates your limiting beliefs, it is your behavior that reinforces them. Likewise, it is your behavior that exposes them.

Why it Matters to You

This is one of the universal truths of life that few understand:

The quality of your thoughts creates the quality of your life.

Aspiring writers think they can't be a great writer, when the world around them is full of great writers. Their limiting beliefs prevent them from seeing this. Aspiring entrepreneurs believe that they cannot become successful entrepreneurs, when the world around them is full of successful entrepreneurs. Their limiting beliefs prevent them from seeing this.
What you think is impossible for you will be impossible. What you think is possible for you could be possible. This does not mean that everything you dream of will come true, it just means that it can be achieved.

- Rewrite the script.
- Change the story you tell yourself.

Reframe your limiting beliefs into enabling beliefs and take small steps in changing your behavior to validate these new beliefs, and you will slowly begin to see how the quality of your thoughts creates the quality of your life.

The limiting belief of "I can't be a writer if I don't have a published book" held me back for a long time until I reformulated it to "I'll write every day and start publishing three articles a week." "

This new belief filled me with the freedom to write frankly.

And then the recurring notion of "who will read my writing" was shattered into pieces as week after week my online readership grew. As I continue to engage in this behavior (writing), I continue to see the many possibilities of what I can accomplish with it.

Your limiting beliefs are self-sabotage.

- Spot them. And then stop them.
- If Eric Weinmayer climbed the highest point on Earth.
- What deters you?

(Answer: your limiting beliefs).

Cultivating the Mindset of a Millionaire

Thinking Like A Millionaire

"If you follow any influencers (or care about social media at all), you've probably heard someone mention the millionaire mentality. It's a staple of hustle culture. People casually mention that you have a millionaire mentality or tell you that you need one, but what exactly does that mean? Is it something people learn on their own?

The millionaire mindset isn't actually about making a million dollars. It's not even about your net worth, living in a New York penthouse, real estate, financial security, or your bank account.

For those who swear by it, the millionaire mindset is about focusing on changing your life — starting from your perspective — to achieve the goals you've always dreamed of achieving. It's no small task either. You should encourage purposeful habits and ways of thinking daily.

The idea is that millionaires live in a place of abundance that allows them to experience more success and confidence. If you want to achieve your goals, you have to start acting as if you have already achieved them. In this field, your success fuels more success.

What are the millionaire mentality habits?

What do you need to do to get a millionaire mentality? Here are 10 "millionaire thinking" habits you should try:

1. Focus on your goals

If you don't have your goals in mind, how are you supposed to reach them? Your goals could be financial growth, solid well-being, a specific career path, or any other dream. Get into the habit of thinking about what you want to achieve. (On average, it takes 66 days to form a habit.)

Once you have your goals in mind, write them down and keep them where you will see them often. They will always be there to remind you of what you are working towards, even on the tough days.

2. Always be comfortable learning

People often need to remember that the world always offers you something to be a beginner in and start over. When working to achieve goals, you may have to switch strategies. Learning to constantly adapt to new changes may help you realize that your practices were not helpful before.

Small skills help as well. Take note of all the new skills you learn and take pride in how you continue to move forward.

3. Put yourself out there

You cannot achieve your goals by not leaving the house or talking to anyone. Communication and paying attention to how you present yourself is essential. If you are trying out for a business presentation, you must be confident while expressing your passion.

People recognize and remember bold, passionate and courageous individuals who speak up for their goals. Networking can help you connect with like-minded individuals who share the same motivation. Making friends at work also turns colleagues into peers, which increases employee engagement.

4. Be patient

It can be frustrating to feel like you're working fast without being rewarded, but don't let that stop you from focusing on what you want in life. You can't change your life in a week. It's okay if you don't achieve your personal development goals when you hoped.

Good things take time, and the fact that things don't always happen when you want them to doesn't mean they never will."

"5. Accept mistakes as soon as they occur

In order to grow and learn, you have to make mistakes. You should not look at mistakes as things to avoid at all costs, but rather as opportunities to learn from them.

Also remember that there is a difference between sloppy mistakes (avoid them) and plans that don't work but it gives you more information and insight to try a new tactic.

Failures represent opportunities to learn about yourself and your team and offer a great way to develop new skills for the future. Instead of dwelling on your mistakes, reflect on them and accept them as you continue to grow.

6. Don't forget to sleep

To do our best work, we need to get a good rest. We all have busy days, but catching up on sleep helps our minds and bodies. It can be easy to stay up late and push ourselves too hard when our to-do list is full, but that's not sustainable.

Even when you think an extra hour of work will get you closer to your goals, it's likely to tire you out even more and hurt your productivity. Next time this happens, make a conscious choice to sleep. Getting a good rest for your body and mind will make you more motivated and ready to start your day.

7. Keep growth in mind

Professional and personal growth is inevitable as you work to achieve your goals. Maintaining a growth mindset during your journey toward success is essential to reminding you of your beginnings.

If your goals are long-term, take the time and review your progress. Not only will you feel a sense of accomplishment, you'll have more motivation as well. If you're feeling frustrated, breaking your goals down into several tasks can make your progress more tangible.

Growth doesn't come overnight and without hard work, which is what I did. Reflecting on your growth will give you a sense of pride that you should cherish.

Businessman wearing a white shirt is sitting and writing a report on a piece of paper

8. Stop making excuses for yourself

Excuses will hold you back from moving forward and achieving your goals. Do you have a problem? Try some time-tested problem-solving techniques. Try to address problems instead of blaming other factors or complaining about your failures.

Work with a trusted coach or mentor to understand what's holding you back or causing you trouble. Focus on making behavioral changes to make a difference for yourself.

Whether that means asking for help, changing your approach, or even taking a break, remember that the worst thing you can do is let your excuses consume you.

9. Learn to invest

When it comes to financial success, the secret to the millionaire mind is simple: Don't lose money. Take your future seriously by prioritizing your financial wellness and setting financial goals that focus on investing rather than spending.

If you need to take financial risks such as allocating capital, you can be confident that the outlay will yield returns. Research and work closely with successful entrepreneurs, and listen to their advice.

10. Adopt a "now" mindset.

While patience is indeed a virtue, one of the habits of wealthy people is to take advantage of new opportunities.

While some of these risks will mean temporary financial losses, there will also be fewer revenue-based opportunities, such as speaking at events and volunteering to help startups.

The more experience you have and the more communication you have, the more opportunities you have to grow personally and professionally.

Business people working together in the office

Cultivate a Growth Mindset Ignite your motivation and build a growth mindset. Our coaches give you the tools to overcome challenges and achieve your goals."

6 professional tips to achieve a millionaire mentality

Everyone wants to know the biggest and most effective tips for achieving a millionaire mindset, but the most important tip to keep in mind is not telling you to buy specific products. They are about cultivating the new lifestyle that this mindset brings you.

1. Believe in yourself

The millionaire mindset is not something you can follow for three days and then reap the benefits forever. It may take longer than you hoped. Believe in your ability to reach your goals one day. Remember, you're doing your best, and that's all you can ask for when you're trying to become the millionaire next door.

2. Be respectful along the way

As you go through this lifestyle change, you are bound to encounter some frustrating times and people. It's okay to feel upset or disappointed, but do your best to be as respectful as possible.

Once you reach your goals, you'll feel more accomplished knowing that you respect everyone who helped you along the way.

3. Turn "I can't" into "I will"

You wouldn't try something if you didn't think you could do it. Predict success for yourself by telling yourself that you will achieve your goals whenever possible. Repeat this positive affirmation every day, often in moments of doubt.

Don't let setbacks deter you, you will achieve your goals, but the path is not linear.

Elegant business woman sitting on balcony and smiling

4. Never trust luck

Confidence and a great career path aren't everything, so always plan for contingencies. Visualize worst-case scenarios, make a plan to deal with them, and work hard to avoid them. For example, times of economic uncertainty mean financial setbacks such as layoffs or recessions.

Save more than your budget requires to make sure you're prepared for anything.

5. Think big!

Creating a clear goal and basing each daily task on progress toward that goal will help you stay motivated and understand why you're working so hard. Remind yourself of this vision when you feel stuck or forget your goal of igniting enthusiasm and energy.

6. Keep love in mind

It's easy to lose sight of what's most important — like your mental health or your relationships — when you're working hard. But your well-being depends on your social health. Research shows that strong social connections are associated with longer lives, less stress, and improved heart health.

Consider friends, family, and coworkers as you work toward your goals. They will inspire you, you will encourage them, and this focus on love will move you forward.

Think like a millionaire

Developing a millionaire mindset is not an overnight process. It involves vision, passion and an incredible amount of hard work. Be patient and insightful, and know that any setbacks are normal and offer a learning experience.

If you are clear about your goals and stay focused, confidence and financial freedom will be within your reach.

Chapter 2: Setting Your Goals

Defining Your Vision For Success

"This article begins a new journey for you, the reader, and for us as well. With this series of editorials we will try to help you create a path that enables you to "Live Your Vision." Exactly what does that mean? From our perspective, living your vision is creating a path in life that enables you to live your best life. The essential step to achieving this is to plan for a safe and comfortable future where you can be financially sound without having to work until the day you leave this earth. The following quote from James Allen, one of the fathers of the self-help movement, provides a perfect summary to consider. "The vision you exalt in your mind, the ideal you crown in your heart—this you will build your life with, and this you will become."

How do you define your journey in this life and your vision of success?

People are looking for ways to tap into magic that will allow them to have the kind of life in which they feel most comfortable. You hear a lot of advice about "the power is within you and you just have to harness it" to achieve this kind of existence. You can meditate, read books, listen to self-help programs, create dream and goal boards, do daily affirmations and still never discover those key first steps that allow you to actually define your vision for your journey through this life.

Start defining your vision as early as possible

It's not too late to start a vision plan. Many people try to figure it out in their 20s if they have a firm grip on the future and what it might bring. However, no matter your age, starting is better than not starting at all! As C.S. Lewis said: "You can't go back and change the beginning, but you can start where you are and change the ending."

Take a moment to figure out what you want from your life and where you want it to go ideally, not just in a financial sense but in a whole life approach. There are some things you should check for yourself to see if you are doing well. Identify the items you need to assemble and decide what type of vision you want to build.

Never be afraid of things that seem impossible. Always take risks.

There should never be a point in your life where you stop daring to take chances. Nothing should seem impossible and you should keep moving forward to achieve things in your professional and personal life. You are your first and best advocate. If you are not pushing yourself to achieve tasks that may seem insurmountable; Nobody will do that.

Failure is a partner to success. Failure builds experience and leads to success.

thomas c. Watson, the man who created the IBM corporate structure, encouraged people not only to keep striving for impossible things, but also to fail, and not just fail, but to view failure as a partner to success. It's something you can grow and learn from and will help clarify the path you want to follow. "Do you want me to give you a formula for success?" Watson asks. "It's very simple, really. Double your failure rate. You think of failure as the enemy of success. But it's not at all. Failure can discourage you or you can learn from it, so go ahead and make mistakes. Make it the best you can. Because Remember, this is where you will find success.

Find the passion and desire to define your vision as your own.

Find the desire that fuels your vision of the present and the future you want to achieve. What's the point of moving forward with a plan and vision if it doesn't spark the desire to succeed within you? It is one of the essential building blocks that allows you to lay the foundation for your future journey in life and money. If you are not passionate about one path and do not have a driving desire to complete that journey and stay on that path; There may be a need to examine how you got on this path in the first place. Has someone else passed their dreams and desires onto you?", "So you accepted their journey as if it was your own? Find your true passion, turn it into your vision, and you will have the motivation and determination to build your current vision and your future vision.

Work hard, strive to excel in your journey, and achieve success.

The ultimate starting point when defining your vision is to strive for excellence in your journey, and work hard to reach success. Success is not something that lies at the end of your vision journey and waits patiently for people to reach for it. Hard work, a good work ethic, being unique about yourself and your way of seeing the present and future are the only ways you will achieve this success. Success does not come to those who are lazy and who sit and wait for an opportunity to knock on the door.", "This article begins a new journey for you, the reader, and for us as well. With this series of editorials we will try to help you create a path that enables you to "Live Your Vision." Exactly what does that mean? From our perspective, living your vision is creating a path in life that enables you to live your best life. The essential step to achieving this is to plan for a safe and comfortable future where you can be financially sound without having to work until the day you leave this earth. The following quote from James Allen, one of the fathers of the self-help movement, provides a perfect summary to consider. "The vision you exalt in your mind, the ideal you crown in your heart—this you will build your life with, and this you will become."

How do you define your journey in this life and your vision of success?

People are looking for ways to tap into magic that will allow them to have the kind of life in which they feel most comfortable. You hear a lot of advice about "the power is within you and you just have to harness it" to achieve this kind of existence. You can meditate, read books, listen to self-help programs, create dream and goal boards, do daily affirmations and still never discover those key first steps that allow you to actually define your vision for your journey through this life.

Start defining your vision as early as possible

It's not too late to start a vision plan. Many people try to figure it out in their 20s if they have a firm grip on the future and what it might bring. However, no matter your age, starting is better than not starting at all! As C.S. Lewis said: "You can't go back and change the beginning, but you can start where you are and change the ending."

Take a moment to figure out what you want from your life and where you want it to go ideally, not just in a financial sense but in a whole life approach. There are some things you should check for yourself to see if you are doing well. Identify the items you need to assemble and decide what type of vision you want to build.

Never be afraid of things that seem impossible. Always take risks.

There should never be a point in your life where you stop daring to take chances. Nothing should seem impossible and you should keep moving forward to achieve things in your professional and personal life. You are your first and best advocate. If you are not pushing yourself to achieve tasks that may seem insurmountable; Nobody will do that.

Failure is a partner to success. Failure builds experience and leads to success.

thomas c. Watson, the man who created the IBM corporate structure, encouraged people not only to keep striving for impossible things, but also to fail, and not just fail, but to view failure as a partner to success. It's something you can grow and learn from and will help clarify the path you want to follow. "Do you want me to give you a formula for success?" Watson asks. "It's very simple, really. Double your failure rate. You think of failure as the enemy of success. But it's not at all. Failure can discourage you or you can learn from it, so go ahead and make mistakes. Make it the best you can. Because Remember, this is where you will find success.

Find the passion and desire to define your vision as your own.

Find the desire that fuels your vision of the present and the future you want to achieve. What's the point of moving forward with a plan and vision if it doesn't spark the desire to succeed within you? It is one of the essential building blocks that allows you to lay the foundation for your future journey in life and money. If you are not passionate about one path and do not have a driving desire to complete that journey and stay on that path; There may be a need to examine how you got on this path in the first place. Has someone else passed their dreams and desires onto you?", "So you accepted their journey as if it was your own? Find your true passion, turn it into your vision, and you will have the motivation and determination to build your current vision and your future vision.

Work hard, strive to excel in your journey, and achieve success.

The ultimate starting point when defining your vision is to strive for excellence in your journey, and work hard to reach success. Success is not something that lies at the end of your vision journey and waits patiently for people to reach for it. Hard work, a good work ethic, being unique about yourself and your way of seeing the present and future are the only ways you will achieve this success. Success does not come to those who are lazy and who sit and wait for an opportunity to knock on the door.", "This article begins a new journey for you, the reader, and for us as well. With this series of editorials we will try to help you create a path that enables you to "Live Your Vision." Exactly what does that mean? From our perspective, living your vision is creating a path in life that enables you to live your best life. The essential step to achieving this is to plan for a safe and comfortable future where you can be financially sound without having to work until the day you leave this earth. The following quote from James Allen, one of the fathers of the self-help movement, provides a perfect summary to consider. "The vision you exalt in your mind, the ideal you crown in your heart—this you will build your life with, and this you will become."

How do you define your journey in this life and your vision of success?

People are looking for ways to tap into magic that will allow them to have the kind of life in which they feel most comfortable. You hear a lot of advice about "the power is within you and you just have to harness it" to achieve this kind of existence. You can meditate, read books, listen to self-help programs, create dream and goal boards, do daily affirmations and still never discover those key first steps that allow you to actually define your vision for your journey through this life.

Start defining your vision as early as possible

It's not too late to start a vision plan. Many people try to figure it out in their 20s if they have a firm grip on the future and what it might bring. However, no matter your age, starting is better than not starting at all! As C.S. Lewis said: "You can't go back and change the beginning, but you can start where you are and change the ending."

Take a moment to figure out what you want from your life and where you want it to go ideally, not just in a financial sense but in a whole life approach. There are some things you should check for yourself to see if you are doing well. Identify the items you need to assemble and decide what type of vision you want to build.

Never be afraid of things that seem impossible. Always take risks.

There should never be a point in your life where you stop daring to take chances. Nothing should seem impossible and you should keep moving forward to achieve things in your professional and personal life. You are your first and best advocate. If you are not pushing yourself to achieve tasks that may seem insurmountable; Nobody will do that.

Failure is a partner to success. Failure builds experience and leads to success.

thomas c. Watson, the man who created the IBM corporate structure, encouraged people not only to keep striving for impossible things, but also to fail, and not just fail, but to view failure as a partner to success. It's something you can grow and learn from and will help clarify the path you want to follow. "Do you want me to give you a formula for success?" Watson asks. "It's very simple, really. Double your failure rate. You think of failure as the enemy of success. But it's not at all. Failure can discourage you or you can learn from it, so go ahead and make mistakes. Make it the best you can. Because Remember, this is where you will find success.

Find the passion and desire to define your vision as your own.

Find the desire that fuels your vision of the present and the future you want to achieve. What's the point of moving forward with a plan and vision if it doesn't spark the desire to succeed within you? It is one of the essential building blocks that allows you to lay the foundation for your future journey in life and money. If you are not passionate about one path and do not have a driving desire to complete that journey and stay on that path; There may be a need to examine how you got on this path in the first place. Has someone else passed their dreams and desires onto you?", "So you accepted their journey as if it was your own? Find your true passion, turn it into your vision, and you will have the motivation and determination to build your current vision and your future vision.

Work hard, strive to excel in your journey, and achieve success.

The ultimate starting point when defining your vision is to strive for excellence in your journey, and work hard to reach success. Success is not something that lies at the end of your vision journey and waits patiently for people to reach for it. Hard work, a good work ethic, being unique about yourself and your way of seeing the present and future are the only ways you will achieve this success. Success does not come to those who are lazy and who sit and wait for an opportunity to knock on the door."

Setting SMART Goals for Financial Growth

What are SMART goals?

SMART goals are the key to achieving your goals on time and with the least amount of stress.

What does SMART stand for? It is an abbreviation that stands for:

- Specific
- Measurable
- Actionable
- Realistic
- Timley

How to write a SMART goal

A great way to think about writing a SMART goal is to check your goals like a good journalist. This means delving into the who, what, where, when, why, and how of each goal you set.

- Who do you set this goal for and who will participate in it?
- What are you trying to achieve with this goal?
- Where will you put your savings for this goal or where do you plan to work on this goal?

- When do you plan to achieve your goal?
- Why is this goal important to you?
- How will you achieve this goal?

Let's break it down...

Step 1: Get specific about your financial goals
Ask yourself: What exactly do I want to achieve? Before you can do anything, you need to be clear about the goals you want to achieve. This is a good time to get into the nitty-gritty of your specific goal so you can understand your intentions behind it.

Here are a few things to take into consideration:

- Who should be involved in your goal and who is your target?
- What are you trying to achieve with this goal?
- Where will you put your money to save toward this financial goal?

So instead of simply saying, "I want to build an emergency fund," say:

I want to save $1,000 in my emergency fund so I can protect my family from unexpected expenses.

Step 2: Track your spending and measure your success
Ask yourself: How will I track my progress and measure my success? Once you've identified your financial goal, now is the time to decide how to track it. What metrics or data will you use to make sure you're on track? Goals are more likely to be followed through if you have ways to measure and monitor your success each month. Ensuring that each of your financial goals is quantifiable and can be identified with clear, hard numbers will make it easier for you to track your progress over time.

Here are a few things to take into consideration:

Set up daily, weekly or monthly reminders on your phone or set up a recurring "money history" alone or with others to review your financial goal and make any necessary revisions

How will you track your success with each check-in?

So instead of simply saying: "I will reach my goal when I save $1,000," say:

I will set up a recurring monthly check-in to review my goal and track my progress.

Step 3: Write actionable steps
Ask yourself: What steps will I take to help me reach this goal? How do you plan to achieve this goal? Create a detailed plan so you can clearly see and understand the steps you need to take each day, week, month and year. What tools, resources or education do you need to help you get started?

Here are a few things to take into consideration:

Do you need to create a separate savings account?
Do you need to automate your savings so you don't have to think about it?
What are some potential obstacles that might come your way and how will you overcome them?

So instead of simply saying, "I'll save $1,000 in my emergency fund," say: I will put $100 into my emergency fund each month to save $1,000.

Step 4: Set realistic financial goals

Ask yourself: Is my goal realistic given my current financial situation? We all have wild dreams for ourselves and that's a good thing! But in order to maintain the motivation necessary to achieve your financial goal, you need to make sure that your goal is realistic and achievable. If you're struggling to save even $50 a month after paying all your bills and expenses, it's unrealistic to think that you can magically start saving $100 a month for an emergency fund. This is a good time to take a hard look at your budget, incoming and outgoing funds, and financial responsibilities. To get an accurate picture of your finances. Only then will you be able to know if this financial goal is realistic for you and your family.

Here are a few things to take into consideration:

Are there places in your budget you can adjust to achieve this goal?
Do you need to adjust your lifestyle to accommodate this goal?
If this financial goal is too unrealistic right now, can you break it down into bite-sized chunks that are achievable right now?

So instead of simply saying, "I will find a way to build my emergency fund," say: I will consider my budget and financial responsibilities when setting this goal.

Step 5: Create a timeline to set goals
Ask yourself: How much time will I give myself to complete this goal? A goal is not a goal until you set yourself a deadline. Once you've determined the who, what, where, why, and how of your financial goal, it's time to determine the when. By setting a deadline to complete a goal, you'll be less likely to procrastinate and hold yourself accountable.

Here are a few things to take into consideration:

Is this a short-term, medium-term, or long-term financial goal?

Don't use the phrases "someday" or "someday" when talking about your goals. Those days will never come if you don't have a clear date in mind.

So instead of simply saying, "One day I will save $1,000 in my emergency fund," say: I will put $100 into my emergency fund each month to save $1,000 in 10 months.

Let's recap our SMART goal setting examples

Specific goal:
I want to save $1,000 in my emergency fund so I can protect my family from unexpected expenses.

Measurable goal:
I will set up a recurring monthly check-in to review my goal and track my progress.

Actionable goal:
I will put $100 into my emergency fund each month to save $1,000.

Realistic goal:
I will consider my budget and financial responsibilities when setting this goal.

Timely target:
I will put $100 into my emergency fund each month to save $1,000 in 10 months.

Setting goals and dreaming about your future can be fun and exciting, but don't let those dreams die through neglect. By creating SMART financial goals, you're setting yourself up for success, and you're more likely to see those dreams become a reality. And don't forget to conduct annual financial check-ins to review your current and financial goals, track your ongoing progress, and celebrate your victories!

If you're having trouble setting smart financial goals for yourself and your family, we can help! Our experienced advisors can guide you through your current financial situation, set achievable short- and long-term goals, adjust your budget, and create a financial action plan to help you move forward. Book your free financial coaching appointment with us today to get started!

Creating a Strategic Plan of Action

Many companies go through strategic planning only to feel that they wasted their time and money, and the process did not lead to any significant change or solutions.

Planning can go awry for many reasons, but one of the most common reasons is a poorly designed or executed business plan. This tool - the basic product of strategic planning - sometimes offers only vague suggestions or lofty goals without clear steps to achieve them. Initiatives may also be unrealistic and developed without team consultation or buy-in.

"The business plan is at the heart of the strategic plan," says Neron Drypaul, a senior business consultant with BDC Advisory Services who advises companies on strategic planning.

"It should provide specific tactical actions that achieve the company's strategic goals. Some strategic plans provide only high-level recommendations without concrete steps. The entrepreneur needs to know exactly what to do next, once the plan is complete."

No plan survives the first contact with reality. The business plan must be constantly updated. Do not continue to work according to a plan that is overtaken by events.

Seven tips for creating a successful business plan.

1. Involve your team early

Your team's participation will make or break the business plan. They should be involved from the beginning during the development of the business plan and other elements of the strategic plan.

"The owner can't do it alone," "Delegation and accountability are key. Some owners try to create a strategic plan themselves and their team doesn't participate. This is the old way, which has a high risk of failure, especially if the owner becomes busy with something else. A good leader gets results." Through teamwork.

Managers involved in strategic planning should brainstorm with their teams what specific projects and steps should be included in the business plan and how to implement them. The idea is to take several great ideas, filter them to select the important ones, create a short list to study them in detail, and then focus on a few key actions that have the greatest potential to help the company achieve its strategic goals and desired future state. .

"The goal is not to make an exhaustive list of everything that needs to be done," says Dryboll. "The idea is to prioritize actions to move from the current state to the desired future state and bridge the gaps between the two."

Involving your team helps ensure that the best ideas are taken into account and that employees participate in implementing them. "The people on the front lines sometimes have the best ideas for planning and execution. You'll get the best team buy-in if as many key employees as possible are involved," says Dryboll.

2. List specific details for each procedure

A business plan is typically presented as a one-page spreadsheet that lists initiatives by function. Actions can be simple one-time projects (for example, hiring a new person), recurring actions (for example, initiating monthly reviews of actual costs versus estimated costs) or a larger project (for example, converting a website to for e-commerce).

For each action, the spreadsheet lists the KPI, the names of those responsible or involved with the initiative, and the timeline for implementation. The spreadsheet may also specify a priority for the initiative (low, medium, or high).

More detailed descriptions of actions usually appear elsewhere in the strategic plan. An action plan is an easy-to-read summary of these initiatives, which your team can use as a quick reference, as well as to track progress.

3. Include a timeline

Business plans generally cover 12 months. For each initiative, the spreadsheet includes a column for each month to list what needs to be done throughout the year. Additional columns are included for each of the remaining quarters of the strategic plan (strategic plans generally cover two to three years in total).

4. Resource allocation

Many business plans are not successful because they do not allocate the appropriate human and financial resources to complete the initiatives. Make sure you allocate enough time, support, training and budgets.

The business plan should be clear about employee responsibilities for each initiative. This can take the form of a RASCI matrix:

Administrator - the one who carries out the work.

Responsible – one who oversees the work, usually the head of the team ("R" and "A" can be the same person, especially in a smaller company).

Support - who provides support.

Consultation – who should be consulted during implementation. For example, a financial manager may need to provide financial information.

Insider – someone who should be informed of progress or decisions, such as a senior person or head of the affected department.

5. Establish a monitoring and measurement process

The action plan must specify the measures necessary to track implementation. These can be milestones (such as completing a task) or quantifiable metrics (such as revenue, margin, or market share).

Also decide how you will follow up on the action plan to ensure the steps are implemented. This can include internal reports and regular meetings to discuss progress. Meetings are often held monthly, with a deeper review conducted quarterly. Meetings help you recognize and reward employees for successes, identify where you're falling behind and examine why so you can take corrective action.

6. Communicate the plan

Ensure that all employees are aware of the work plan and their role in implementing it. Explain its benefits to employees and the organization.

"It is important for your team to know that the business plan is the tactical component of your overall business strategy, which aims to improve company performance,"

"They need to hear it from management and see the connections. People may resist change, but they need to be told that change is inevitable and necessary for the company to survive and thrive. They need to be reassured that the plan will not lead to complete disruption and that it will happen step by step. You need To address people's concerns and make them feel comfortable with the changes.

7. Keep the plan alive

The business plan is not written in stone. It should be flexible, flexible and responsive to issues that arise in implementation and changes in the external and internal landscape. You may need to review actions, priorities, or even your larger goals. Regularly ask for feedback from your team.

"No plan survives its first contact with reality," says Dryboll. "The business plan must be constantly updated. Do not continue to work on a plan that has been overtaken by events."

As the year comes to a close, start talking with your team about developing a new business plan for the next 12 months, based on the lessons you've learned.

"Discussing your business plan regularly is a good way to keep your strategic plan alive and at the forefront of everyone's minds,". "Talk about it where you can. Make each team member accountable for the actions they had to take. You want the plan to become part of everyone's daily work and not be interpreted as a special project to work on when you have extra time.

Chapter 3: Taking Action

Building Momentum with Consistent Action

CONSISTENCY is the key to life – Build your MOMENTUM!

Sometimes it hurts me to think about how much effort it takes to get momentum. Creating momentum is everything in life and business, but the consistency needed to gain momentum is why 99% of people fail to achieve their goals. Consistency is what makes champions. Consistency is the difference between professionals and amateurs. Consistency requires us to break through laziness over and over again, a million times over, until the momentum of our creativity becomes unstoppable. Too many people in this world are blinded by the pursuit of comfort and completely satisfied with mediocrity. There's nothing wrong with this lazy lifestyle, and this blog isn't meant to energize unmotivated people. This blog is aimed at dreamers. It is for people who have the spark in their souls that is bound to set the world on fire. You have the potential to achieve great things in this world, but do you have the drive to turn that potential into momentum? The answer is yes, but you must overcome your laziness and find the power of consistency if you want to succeed.

CONSISTENCY IS A MINDSTATE

The first thing to understand when creating momentum for your life or business is that consistency is a state of mind. It's not a special skill you need to learn or train, it's literally the ability to get off your ass and go do some work. It is essential that your end goal is firmly visualized in your mind so that it is consistent. Know what your goals are and draw the entire picture of success in your mind. Since I'm a musician and write mostly about the music industry, I think it makes sense to use music as an example. If you want to become a professional musician, your vision for success must be completely mapped out. Success may mean something different to everyone. Some musicians want to become global stars like Michael Jackson, others will be happy simply making an honest living playing their instruments. Whatever your goals are, keep them clearly defined in your mind so you can link goals back to the actions needed to achieve them. In this example, consistency might mean playing your instrument every day, no matter what. Are you tired? Are you sick? Do you personally spend a day just relaxing? Momentum doesn't care about your personal day. Momentum pays attention to consistency, effort and results. As you relax about your personal day, I guarantee there will be another musician constantly practicing their art and ready to take your place.

SUCCESS
IT IS THE SUM OF EFFORTS
REPEATED
DAY IN DAY OUT

MOMENTUM FUELS MOTIVATION

The best thing about momentum is that when it finally hits you can feel it in your soul! Nothing will fuel your motivation more than momentum. It has the ability to dramatically multiply the results of everything you do, which will naturally make you want to do more! Take a second to imagine if you have traction here within the #steemit blogging community. If you were making hundreds of dollars every time you posted a blog here, wouldn't you get off your ass and be more consistent with your efforts? Hell yeah you will! And imagine what? It's possible through the power of consistency!

Keep pushing forward my friends! I want you all to feel the energy that momentum can bring to your life.

The Law Of Momentum

A moving object will remain in motion until it encounters a resisting force. Keep pushing forward

Overcoming Procrastination And Fear

Why do so many people procrastinate and how do you overcome it?

For most people, procrastination, no matter what they say, is not about laziness. In fact, when we procrastinate, we often work intensely for long periods before our deadlines. Working long and hard is the opposite of laziness, so that can't be the reason we do it. So why do we procrastinate, and more importantly, what can we do about it?

As suggested above, some say they procrastinate because they are lazy. Others claim that they "work better" when they procrastinate and "work better" under pressure. I encourage you to be critical and reflective of these interpretations. Almost everyone who says this is usually procrastinating and has not completed an important academic assignment in which they made a plan, executed it, had time to review, etc. before the deadline. So, in reality, they cannot make a comparison about the conditions under which they work best. If you pretty much always procrastinate, and never approach your tasks systematically, you won't be able to accurately say that you know you "do better" under pressure. Still other people say that they like the "rush" of leaving things to the end and meeting the deadline. But they usually say this when they are not working on that deadline. They say this works well before or after starting school when they forget the negative consequences of procrastination such as feelings of anxiety, stress, fatigue, and disappointment from falling below their own standards and having to put their lives on hold for long periods of time. Not to mention, leaving things to the end greatly increases the chances that something will go wrong – such as illness or a computer problem – and you won't be able to get your desired grade. So, procrastinating can be hard on us and actually increases our chances of failure, but we do it anyway. How is that?

"**Procrastination** is not limited to poor time management skills, but can be traced back to underlying and more complex psychological causes. These dynamics are often exacerbated by schools where students are constantly evaluated, especially at colleges where the pressure for grades is high and much can depend on student performance. In fact, procrastination is often a self-protection strategy for students. For example, if you procrastinate, you always have the excuse of "not having enough time" in case you fail, so your sense of ability is never threatened. When there is a lot of pressure to get a good grade, for example, in a research paper, it is no wonder that students want to avoid it and thus postpone their work. Most often, our reasons for delaying and avoiding are rooted in fear and anxiety — about doing poorly, doing too well, losing control, looking stupid, or challenging one's sense of self or self-concept. We avoid doing work to avoid judgment of our abilities. If we succeed, we feel "smarter." So, what can we do to overcome our tendencies to procrastinate?

Awareness: The First Step

First, to overcome procrastination, you must have an understanding of the reasons you procrastinate and the function procrastination performs in your life. You can't come up with an effective solution if you don't really understand the root of the problem. As with most problems, awareness and self-knowledge are the keys to knowing how to stop procrastinating. For many people, gaining this insight into how procrastination protects them from feeling like they're not capable enough, and keeping that in mind when they tend to fall into familiar, unproductive habits and procrastinate goes a long way to solving the problem. For example, psychologists Jane Burka and Lenora Yuen, who have helped many people overcome procrastination, state in their article "The Mind Games Procrastinators Play" (Psychology Today, January 1982), that many students "understand the hidden roots of procrastination ". Procrastination often seems to weaken them" (p. 33). Simply knowing the real reasons for procrastination makes it easier to stop.

Time management techniques: one piece of the puzzle

To overcome procrastination, time management techniques and tools are indispensable, but they are not sufficient in themselves. Not all time management techniques are equally useful in dealing with procrastination. There are some time management techniques that are perfectly suitable for overcoming procrastination and others that can make it worse. Those that reduce anxiety and fear and emphasize the satisfaction and rewards of completing tasks are best. Those that are inflexible, emphasize the size of tasks and increase anxiety, can actually increase procrastination, and thus be counterproductive. For example, making a huge list of "things to do" or scheduling every minute of your day may increase your stress and thus procrastinate. Instead, set reasonable goals (for example, a manageable list of things to do), break down larger tasks, give yourself flexibility and make time for things you enjoy as a reward for work done."

Motivation: Finding productive reasons to engage in tasks

To overcome procrastination, it is important to stay motivated for productive reasons. By productive reasons, I mean reasons for learning and achievement that lead to positive, productive, and satisfying feelings and actions. These reasons contrast with engaging in a task out of fear of failure, not pissing off your parents, not looking stupid, or doing better than others in order to "show off." While these are all reasons – often very powerful ones – to do something, they are not productive because they trigger maladaptive, often negative, feelings and actions. For example, if you are concerned about not looking stupid, you may not ask questions, delve into new areas, try new methods, or take the risks necessary to learn new things and reach new heights. A good way to trigger positive motivation is to set your goals and focus on them. Identify and write down your personal reasons for enrolling in the course and monitor your progress towards your goals with a goal setting planner. Remember to focus on your why and goals. Other people's goals for you are not goals at all, but obligations.

Stay Motivated: Be energized to participate

Another key to overcoming procrastination is to stay actively involved in your classes. If you are passive in class, you are probably not "getting into" the course and its topics, and this saps your motivation. What's more, if you're passive, you're probably not understanding the course and its materials as much as you could. Nonsense and confusion are not attractive; In fact, it is boring and frustrating. We don't often want to do things that are boring or frustrating. Prevent this by aiming to truly understand the material, not memorize it or just "pass" it. Instead, try (1) looking for what is interesting and relevant to you in the course materials, (2) setting your own purpose for each reading and study session, and (3) asking yourself (and others) questions about what you are learning.

Summary of tips to overcome procrastination

Awareness – Think about the reasons you procrastinate and your habits and thoughts that lead to procrastination.

Evaluation – What emotions lead to procrastination, and how does it make you feel? Are these feelings positive and productive: do you want to change them?

Outlook - Change your perspective. Looking at a big task in terms of small parts makes it less intimidating. Find what attracts you, or what you want to get out of the job other than just the grade.

Commit – If you feel stuck, start by simply committing to completing a small task, any task, and write it down. Complete it and reward yourself. Write in your schedule or "to do" list only what you can absolutely commit to, and if you write it down, follow through no matter what. By doing this, you will slowly rebuild confidence in yourself that you will actually do what you say you will do, which is what many procrastinators have lost.

Surroundings – When doing schoolwork, choose wisely where you work and with whom. Frequently putting yourself in situations where you don't get much done — such as "studying" in your bed, at a café, or with friends — can actually be a form of procrastination, a way to avoid work.

Goals – Focus on what you want to do, not what you want to avoid. Think about productive reasons to do a task by setting positive, tangible, and meaningful learning and achievement goals for yourself.

Be realistic – achieving goals and changing habits takes time and effort; Don't sabotage yourself by setting unrealistic expectations that you can't meet.

Self-talk – Notice how you think and talk to yourself. Talk to yourself in ways that remind you of your goals and replace old, counterproductive self-talk habits. Instead of saying, "I wish I didn't..." say, "I will..."

Eliminate your schedule – If you feel stuck, you probably won't use a schedule that is a constant reminder of everything you have to do and is all work and no play. So, set up a flexible, largely unstructured schedule in which you only identify what is necessary. Track any time you spend working toward your goals and reward yourself for it. This can reduce feelings of exhaustion and increase satisfaction with what you accomplish.

Leveraging Your Strengths and Resources

Sarah's first job as a leader

Since she was a child, Sarah has been a natural leader. You love bringing people together and brainstorming ideas.

So, when she was hired to lead the marketing team, she was excited. But as she got into the details of the job, she realized that everything that needed to be done was not in her strength.

She was not good at putting together detailed agendas and making sure meetings stayed on topic. She was better at brainstorming and sharing ideas with her team. But she didn't want to let her team down, so she found a way to make it work. She delegated the agenda to someone on her team who was good at it and focused on leadership instead.

The team came up with great ideas and Sarah felt good about her role. Everyone was successful.

Focus on what you do well

We all have equal help in terms of strengths and weaknesses. However, we tend to focus on our weaknesses.

What would happen if you instead played to your strengths? It can be easy to get caught up in trying to improve areas where you're struggling, but it's important to take time to focus on what you're doing well. When you focus on what you do well, you'll be able to build on those skills and use them as a foundation for success.

Just as it takes time and effort to clearly understand your weaknesses, understanding your strengths also takes time and effort. But once you do, you'll know what sets you apart and you can make the most of those strengths to achieve success that only you can achieve.

Five Steps to Leverage Your Strengths

Identify your strengths. The first step to leveraging your strengths is to identify what they are. Think about the things you are naturally good at and enjoy doing. These are your strengths. If you're not sure what your strengths are, ask a friend or family member for input.

Find a role that suits your strengths. Focus on your natural talents. Once you know what your strengths are, you can start looking for roles that fit them. For example, if you are a people person, you may want to consider a role in customer service or sales. If you are good at solving problems, you may want to consider a role in research or analysis.

Use your strengths to your advantage. Once you find a role that fits your strengths, it's time to start using them to your advantage. Play to your strengths in everything you do and look for opportunities to use your strengths as much as possible. The more you use your strengths, the better you will become at them and the more successful you will be.

Don't be afraid to ask for help. Even when you're good at something, you still need help sometimes. It's okay to communicate and you won't succeed if you don't. When you find yourself struggling, find someone with more experience and ask them for help.

Continue to develop your strengths. Never stop expanding your strengths. The world is always changing, and so are the skills required. By maintaining your current strengths and expanding into new areas, you will have the skills needed to remain successful. Celebrate your successes, no matter how small.

"Do not be afraid of your talents. They were made for use. What is a sundial in the shadows?"

Identifying your strengths promotes self-awareness but also helps you succeed in whatever you choose to do in life. This could mean your relationships, hobbies, and in the workplace. The first step is to be able to understand the different types of strengths you have and then how you can leverage them to achieve success.

The word strength has several meanings. To understand the concept of strengths and define your self-awareness, you need to recognize the three different types of strengths and the basis they have in your success.

Identify strengths:

Step 1: Skills

The first type of power is your personal skills. These are things that can be easily taught through demonstration. They can be things that come naturally to you too. Some skills may be difficult at first for some, but with repetition, they can be acquired. Such as riding a bike, driving a car, etc. Some examples of workplace skills are:

- Written communication
- Public speaking
- Time management
- Verbal communication
- Networks

Step 2: Behaviors and personality traits

The next step is to know your behavioral strengths. These behaviors build from your first basic skills. So what behaviors affect the way you ride a bike or car? Some examples of behaviors are:

- Receptive to comments and criticism
- Flexibility
- Trustworthy and accountable
- Determination
- Adaptable

Step 3: Attitudes and Beliefs

These stem from the second step of behaviors and personality traits as well. Attitudes and beliefs reinforce and set limits to the development of your behaviors and skills. This can come from experiences, religion, societal norms, and more. Some examples of attitudes and beliefs are:

- People deserve kindness and respect
- Hope
- Believing that people are good
- Believing that feedback supports your growth
- Believing that you have the strength to let go of everything life has to offer

What would you like to do?

After you can dig deep and know your three core strengths, you can leverage them into whatever you want to do in life and/or your career. Next, you need to know what your passion is.

Step 4: Identify your emotions

This step is crucial because identifying your strengths is only great if you are directing them towards your dreams. This way you will achieve the most success in whatever you choose to do in your life and career. Some examples of emotions are:

- Working with people
- The Animals
- Technology
- Films/Production
- Writing
- A Job
- Create
- Art
- Decide what comes next.

Step 5: Figure out what you want to do

What do you want to do with this information you learned about yourself? Do you want to start a career? Do you want to do something besides your day job? Now is the time to figure out what you want to do with your life, skills, and passions and figure out what you need to do to get there.

- Do you need to go back to school?
- Do you need to start a business on the side?
- Do you need to save money?
- What do you need to do to leverage your strengths and channel them into your passion?
- How will you get there?

Chapter 4: Mastering Money Management

Over the past five years, I have tried and tested many strategies to manage my money effectively. Understanding how to control your money is a crucial life skill, regardless of your income level. Whether you make $50,000 or $100,000 a year, the key is how you manage your money.

The real skill of money management is making the most of the money you have, striking a balance between living in the present and planning for the future. Managing your money doesn't have to seem like a daunting task. It should be easy to do and easy to maintain.

I want to share with you my three-step method for managing your money effectively and feeling in complete control of your financial situation. I'll also share some of my favorite tips along the way.

Step 1: Identify the three elements

The first step to taking control of your money is deciding where you want to allocate it. Before you do that, you need to determine exactly how much money you bring home each month — the amount that makes it into your bank account after taxes and deductions.

If you have multiple sources of income, be sure to include them all. Whether it's your 9-5 job, weekend gig, freelancing, or investments, list them all in the income section. This gross income will serve as the basis for your financial planning.

Once you calculate your total income, you can distribute it into the three main groups: basic, fund, and future. The basic bucket covers your basic needs, while the fund bucket includes costs that bring joy and experiences into your life. Finally, the Future Bucket represents investments in the life you envision for the future.

Step 2: Track your spending

It's important to track your spending in three columns: essentials, fun stuff, and future. The essentials column includes non-negotiable expenses such as housing, utilities, transportation, groceries, insurance, and debt payments.

The Fun Stuff column is about discretionary spending — subscriptions, entertainment, dining out, shopping, and other discretionary expenses that enrich your life. The "Future You" column is for paying yourself first, investing in stocks, adding to your emergency fund, and saving for specific goals.

By tracking your spending in each category and comparing it to the percentages included in your budget, you can adjust your financial priorities accordingly.

Step 3: Reflect and adapt

At the end of each month, think about your spending habits. Did you pay all your bills on time? Are there areas you have overspent or not saved? Determine the reasons for any discrepancies and make adjustments as needed.

By constantly tracking and reflecting on your financial habits, you can improve your overall financial health and stay on track toward achieving your money management goals.

Understanding The Flow Of Money

There's a lot to consider when it comes to cash flow management. Without the right knowledge, business owners can make critical mistakes. I'll demystify the complexities of cash flow, and guide you through its pivotal role in maintaining and growing your business.

What is cash flow in business?

In business, cash flow relates to the ebb and flow of cash resources within a company. It serves as a vital backbone that enables seamless business operations, including the ability to cover payroll, inventory purchasing, and fuel expansion initiatives.

Positive cash flow indicates a company's ability to maintain its operations, while negative cash flow can be a warning sign of impending financial challenges.

Therefore, skillfully managing cash flow is a crucial factor for business success. Inadequate cash flow management can push a company into bankruptcy, regardless of its profitability.

The main components of cash flow

To understand the main components of cash flow, it is necessary to distinguish between cash inflow and cash outflow. This distinction is intricately related to the roles that operations, investing, and financing activities play in cash flow management.

Cash Inflow

Cash flow is the flow of money entering a business. Primary sources include revenue from sales, which is the core of most enterprises. In addition, companies may also receive money from investments, loans, and sometimes grants or subsidies. These flows are necessary to cover daily operations and future investments.

Cash Outflows

Cash outflow represents money leaving the business. This includes operating expenses such as rent, salaries, payments to suppliers for goods or services, loan repayments, and obligations such as taxes and debt service. Managing outflows is critical to maintaining financial solvency and ensuring business continuity.

The importance of cash flow management

Effective financial management is the cornerstone of business sustainability. Improper management will have its consequences. However, sound management ensures smooth operations, informed decisions, and protection from unexpected financial challenges.

Let's dive deeper into understanding positive and negative cash flows and strategies on how to deal with them.

Positive cash flow

Positive cash flow occurs when a company receives more money than it spends. The benefits are multifaceted: they provide sufficient cash reserves, ensure solvency, and create the potential for reinvestment and growth.

Here are some basic strategies for increasing positive cash flow:

- Issuing invoices and collecting payments in a timely manner
- Effective expense management
- Offer incentives for early payments
- Increase sales and revenues
- Expanding the customer base through marketing efforts
- Diversify sources of income

Negative cash flow

Negative cash flow occurs when a company's cash expenses exceed its earnings. This situation can have serious repercussions, including difficulty covering regular expenses, accumulating debt, and restricting funds for growth initiatives and investments. Continuing negative cash flow may also tarnish a company's reputation and creditworthiness.

Here's how to navigate and possibly reverse a negative cash flow situation:

- Extend repayment terms or establish staggered repayment plans to ease immediate financial burdens.

- Review and eliminate or reduce unnecessary expenses, with a focus on improving operational efficiency.

- Consider short-term loans or lines of credit to bridge the cash flow gap and ensure continued operation.

How to manage cash flow effectively

Although the intricacies of cash flow management can be complex, having a solid understanding of its basics and maintaining constant monitoring can be a game-changer. As we delve deeper, let's explore key strategies and useful tools that can help business owners navigate fluctuations in their finances.

Cash flow forecasting and analysis

Cash flow forecasting and budgeting are essential elements of effective management. It enables companies to identify potential cash flow problems in advance and make wise choices for their financial operations.

To improve cash flow, consider techniques such as creating detailed cash flow forecasts and regularly monitoring and adjusting forecasts based on actual performance. This proactive approach ensures you can address cash flow challenges before they become critical.

Working capital and inventory management

Working capital management and inventory levels greatly impact cash flow. Improving inventory levels and streamlining accounts receivable and payable processes can free up cash that may be tied up in excess inventory or late payments.

Implementing effective working capital practices ensures that your company has the liquidity needed to meet its short-term obligations and invest in growth.

Access to external financing options

In times of cash flow constraints, access to external financing options is critical. Short-term financing options such as lines of credit or business loans can provide a quick infusion of capital to fill cash flow gaps.

It is essential to explore these options and establish relationships with financial institutions to have a safety net when cash flow challenges arise.

Tools and techniques for monitoring cash flow

After discussing the importance of managing your cash flow, let's explore some tools and techniques to effectively monitor your company's finances:

Cash flow statements
Cash flow statements provide a detailed breakdown of how money moves in and out of a company over a specific period. This financial document is invaluable, providing a snapshot of a company's liquidity and its ability to maintain operations, debt service and financing expansions.

Accounting programs
Modern accounting software simplifies financial management, providing real-time insights into cash flow. These tools automate invoicing, track expenses, and create financial reports, making it easier for business owners to monitor their financial health.

Regular financial analysis and review

Continuous analysis and review of financial statements is crucial. This practice helps identify trends, predict potential challenges, and measure overall company performance. Regular reviews ensure that companies remain proactive, adjusting strategies based on the current financial situation and market conditions.

Mastering the Cash Stream: A Brief Guide to Budgeting Business Finances

In the complex symphony of business operations, cash flow management takes center stage as a wise practice. Throughout this article, we cover the basic concepts of cash inflow and outflow, explain the implications of positive and negative cash flow, and reveal indispensable tools for monitoring the financial ebbs and flows. To avoid any critical mistakes when running your business, keep these ideas in mind as you continue your business endeavors.

FAQs

What is free cash flow in a business?
Free cash flow represents the cash a company generates after accounting for capital expenditures. It is an indicator of a company's financial flexibility, showing funds available for dividends, debt repayment and reinvestment.

Is cash flow the same as profit?
No, cash flow and profits are different. While profit measures total revenues minus total expenses during a period, cash flow examines the net amount of cash that moves in and out. It is possible for a company to be profitable but have negative cash flow, and vice versa.

What is good cash flow for small businesses?
A good small business cash flow is one in which inflows consistently exceed outflows, allowing for operating expenses and growth investments. The exact amount can vary based on the industry, business model and growth stage.

What is net cash flow in a business?

Net cash flow is the difference between cash inflows and outflows during a specific period. Positive net cash flow means that the company generated more cash than it spent, while negative net cash flow indicates the opposite.

How to analyze cash flows?

Cash flow analysis involves reviewing cash flow statements, classifying cash activities (operating, investing, and financing), and examining trends. Key metrics such as operating cash flow margin, free cash flow, and cash conversion cycle can help assess financial health and efficiency.

Implementing Effective Budgeting Strategies

An office employee signs papers on a desk near a laptop.
Budgeting is an important personal and professional skill for people in many industries. It helps you ensure financial stability and allows you to facilitate the growth of a company. Learning effective budgeting strategies can help you manage your finances and improve your financial skills to advance your career.
I explain what a budget strategy is, list several budget strategies to consider and provide tips for maintaining your budget.
Strengthen your profile
What are your desired job types?
Full-time
Part-time
Contract
Temporary

What is a budget strategy?
A budget strategy is a formal approach to managing a collection of funds. Many people use budget strategies in their personal lives to ensure their expenses don't exceed their

income. Others use budgeting strategies to help reach financial goals, like purchasing a new car or saving a certain amount for retirement. Many professionals also use budgeting strategies at work to help ensure a department or organization can pay for all its expenses and potentially invest in future opportunities.

You can try several budgeting strategies to find one that best aligns with your goals and needs. Here's a list of 12 effective budget strategies you can use to reach your financial objectives:

1. Subtraction budgeting
Subtraction budgeting is one of the simplest forms of budgeting. To use this method, you add all your monthly expenditures and subtract that total from your overall monthly earnings. The amount you have left over is what you can use for savings and entertainment.

2. Cash budgeting
Cash budgeting, which some people call envelope budgeting, has you use actual cash for purchases and expenses instead of managing digital currency. Having cash often helps those who have trouble imagining their money in digital form track it more easily.
With a cash budgeting system, rather than putting your paycheck into your bank account, you cash it and use the physical bills and coins to pay for your expenses. Some people put the specific amount of cash they need for expenses, like rent and utilities, into sealed envelopes until they pay those bills, so they can avoid spending it on other things.

3. Proportional budgeting
With a proportional budgeting strategy, you divide all your expenditures into three categories, which are savings, needs and wants. From there, you determine which percentage of your income you want to dedicate to each of these categories. Then, you can divide your income into those categories accordingly.

4. Two-bank budgeting

Using the two-bank budgeting strategy, you pay yourself before paying any other expenses. This allows you to add to any savings plans or purchase any items you want. One effective method of this strategy is to open a checking account in which you deposit your paycheck. Then, set up an automatic transfer from that account to a secondary bank account, leaving a small portion of your paycheck behind in the original account. You then can live off the money in your secondary account and leave the savings from your original account for emergencies or other purchasing goals.

5. Automatic budgeting

Automatic budgeting allows you to benefit from the built-in budgeting systems many banks provide. Consider setting up automatic bill pay and automatic transfers. This ensures you pay all your expenses on time and meet your savings goals without having to make any actual payments or deposits.

6. Online or app budgeting

Many applications help you track your spending and effectively create a personalized budget that meets your goals and needs. Budget applications are software applications that sync to your financial accounts and aggregate all your information in one place, so you always know the amount of money you're spending and earning. Consider using one of these programs to help you establish a unique budgeting system specifically for you and your spending patterns.

7. 50/30/20 budgeting

The 50/30/20 system is a traditional budgeting strategy that uses ratios to help you manage your money. Essentially, with this strategy, 50% of your income goes to your needs or non-negotiable essentials, like rent and utilities, 30% goes to your wants or personal expenses, like dinners out and other entertainment, and 20% goes toward savings and paying off any debt you have. People who want to buy a property or create an emergency savings account can benefit from using the 50/30/20 budgeting strategy.

8. Multi-account budgeting

The multi-accounting budgeting system is a digital version of the cash envelope budgeting strategy. Using this system, you open multiple bank accounts and dedicate each to a specific expenditure or savings goal. You can use automatic transfers to send the appropriate amount of money to each account and automatic bill pay programs to ensure you pay your expenses on time.

9. Zero-based budgeting

A zero-based budgeting approach is another traditional strategy that focuses on ensuring you have enough of your income set aside to cover your necessary expenses. With this method, you subtract expenditures from your monthly income until you have a remainder that fully funds whatever is most important that month. This means you're working toward a zero-waste situation with your funds, ensuring you account for all of your income.

10. Savings and emergency budgeting

If you want to maximize your savings, a savings and emergency budgeting strategy may be highly effective. With this method, a certain percentage of your income goes into a general savings account you can use for specific purchasing goals, like a house or a car. Another percentage goes into an emergency fund for unexpected expenses, like a car repair or loss of a job.

11. Prepaid debit card budgeting

A strategic budgeting approach for those who dislike carrying cash but struggle to limit their credit card use is the prepaid debit card budgeting strategy. It functions as a combination of the cash envelope system and the multi-account budgeting strategy, but it uses prepaid debit cards for daily expenses instead of using cash or a card for your bank account. This ensures you can't overdraw your account and spend outside of your means.

12. Priority budget

A priority budget includes determining your priorities instead of relying on predetermined priorities others set. You make a list of all your expenses and spending priorities and arrange them in the order that's most important to you. From there, you can determine how much money you want to dedicate to each category.

Deciding on a budget strategy is an excellent first step in effectively saving your money. Ensuring you follow the guidelines you establish in your budget can help you meet your short- and long-term budgeting goals. Here are a few tips to help you maintain your budget:

Track spending. One of the best ways to maximize your budget is to track your spending and see where you can make changes to meet your short- and long-term financial goals.

Review and update. Regularly review the budget you've created to ensure you're spending within the limits. Update and change your budget as needed to reflect spending patterns and changing goals.

Establish goals. Ensure the goals you set for your budget are realistic and attainable. Consider using the SMART goals to help you create effective financial goals.
Use tools. Use tools like apps and online money trackers to help you get a clear sense of your spending and saving.

Stay motivated. Regularly remind yourself why you're using a budget by looking at your long-term goals to help you stay motivated to save.

Reduce credit card use. It can be easy to overspend with a credit card. If you often accrue unnecessary credit card debt, consider using cash or debit cards instead to keep you from spending more money than you have.

Investing Wisely for Long-Term Growth

When you have more money and no urgent needs, one or two things most people think about is investing. But investment is not always profitable, especially long-term investment.

There are many factors that need to be considered and known so that long-term investments can be made correctly and wisely and bring benefits.
For those of you who are still classified as beginners in terms of investment, this article may be for you. Don't miss some important information that will make your long-term investment more profitable and rewarding.

Tips and types of long-term investments to choose wisely

What is long term investment?
In general, long-term investing is a financial strategy that involves putting money away for a relatively long and extended period, usually more than five years.
It takes certain concepts to select the right type of long-term investment, so that the main goals of long-term investment can be well achieved.

What is the purpose of long-term investing?
Preparing for retirement funds
Many individuals use long-term investing as a way to prepare for retirement. By starting long-term investments early, they can harness the power of long-term growth to create strong financial stability in retirement.

Preparing for children's education

When having children, one of the things that parents should think about is their children's future education. No wonder parents often start making long-term investments to ensure adequate funds for their children's education. Long time horizons allow investors to ride out market volatility and achieve their targeted learning goal.

Raising capital to purchase real estate

Long-term investments can be used to raise the capital needed to purchase real estate. This could include residential homes or investments in commercial real estate.

Capital Growth

One of the goals of long-term investing is capital growth, where long-term investments are made to increase the value of the investment over time. This provides an opportunity for investors to make significant gains through appreciation of the asset value.

Types Of Long-term Investment

1. Stocks

Stock investing is the purchase of shares or partial ownership of a company's shares. When someone buys a stock, they are buying a small piece of ownership in that company. Shares are traded on a stock market, and their value can change over time based on a variety of factors, including company performance, economic conditions, and market sentiment.

Owning company shares offers the potential for significant capital growth. Stocks are suitable for investors who are willing to tolerate short-term market volatility in favor of long-term returns.

While investing in stocks can offer the potential for great returns, it also involves a high degree of risk. Therefore, it is important to have a good understanding of the company you are investing in, conduct market research, and have an investment plan that suits your personal goals and risk tolerance. Many investors also consult with a financial professional before making major investment decisions.

2. Bonds

Bonds are debt securities issued by companies or governments. They provide a fixed income in the form of interest and are suitable for investors looking for stability and regular income.

Bond investing involves purchasing bonds as a form of equity participation. Bonds are financial instruments issued by governments, companies, or other entities to borrow money from investors. In bond investing, an investor who buys a bond gives a loan to the bond issuer for a specified period at a specified interest rate.

The market price of a bond can fluctuate depending on factors such as changes in interest rates, economic conditions, and the credit rating of the bond issuer. Bond prices can be higher, lower, or equal to the face value.

In addition, bonds are given a credit rating by credit rating agencies to measure the credit risk of the issuer. This rating can affect the interest rate offered by the bond and the risk of the investment.

3. Mutual Fund

A mutual fund is a pool of money from different investors managed by an investment manager. This allows portfolio diversification and risk management.

In this regard, in practical terms, mutual funds are investment vehicles that pool money from several investors to invest in different types of assets, such as stocks, bonds, and money market instruments. Professional investment managers manage a mutual fund portfolio according to predetermined investment objectives, and profits or losses from the investment are shared according to each investor's ownership percentage.

Mutual fund investments are suitable for investors who want to engage in the financial markets without having to directly manage their portfolios. Before investing in mutual funds, it is important to understand the investment objectives, risks and costs involved and conduct research to choose a mutual fund that suits your investment profile.

4. Real estate/real estate

Real estate investing is investing in physical real estate, such as apartments or commercial properties, that can provide long-term growth in value as well as rental income. It is suitable to be enjoyed in retirement.

Technically, long-term investing in real estate or property involves acquiring, owning and managing property with the aim of benefiting from increases in property value, rental income, or both.

One of the main goals of long-term real estate investing is to benefit from the property's increasing value over time. Location, surrounding infrastructure, and economic development of the area can affect the potential increase in property value.

In addition, real estate investments can provide regular income through rent. Property owners can earn monthly or annual income from renting their real estate units to tenants.

5. Precious metals

Long-term investing in precious metals refers to the practice of storing and holding precious metal assets, such as gold, silver, platinum, or palladium, for a longer period in the hope that the value of the investment will increase over time.

Precious metals are often considered a relatively stable form of investment and can act as a hedge against currency fluctuations and economic uncertainty. For example, precious metals, especially gold, are often considered a form of hedge against inflation and economic instability. Long-term investments in precious metals can help prevent a decline in the purchasing power of the currency.

Keep in mind that long-term investments in any field require a deep understanding of risk factors, market knowledge, and long-term financial planning. By choosing the right investment vehicle, investors can achieve their financial goals and build strong financial resources over time.

Tips for Safe and Successful Long-Term Investing

For those of you who want to start a safe long-term investment, don't miss these tips:

1. Understand risk factors

Know your risk factor by choosing an investment that suits your comfort level with market fluctuations. Don't forget that every investment has risks, and understanding those risks is key to making wise decisions.

2. Long-term investment options

Choosing appropriate investment tools for the long term, such as shares of companies that have long-term growth potential. This helps you overcome market fluctuations that may occur in the short term.

So, do your research so you can choose the best investment instrument. Conduct thorough research on the company or investment vehicle you are considering. Look at the company's financial performance, growth prospects, and management.

3. Reinvest profits

If you invest in stocks that pay dividends, consider reinvesting the dividends. This allows you to take advantage of the benefits of compound interest and increase your long-term growth potential.

Although it is a long-term investment, it is important to monitor your investment regularly. Conduct periodic reviews to ensure that the investment is still in line with your financial goals.

4. Mature financial planning

Set long-term financial goals and create an investment plan accordingly. Careful financial planning helps you stay focused on your goals and avoid rash decisions.

5. Do not hesitate to consult a specialist

If possible, consider consulting a financial professional. They can help you plan an investment strategy that fits your goals and financial situation.

Keep in mind that any investment always involves risk, and financial volatility can vary. Therefore, understanding your investments well, being wise, patient and having a long-term perspective are key to safely achieving your long-term investment goals.

PLAN NOW
Financial calculator
Find the solution

Chapter 5: Sales Mastery

Unleashing Your Sales Potential

"Unleash your sales potential" can still be a great slogan, or it can be your reality. If you're serious about sales success and want to make it happen, take some time to ask yourself 10 key questions. The answers to these questions will provide greater awareness of where you stand today, reveal the internal and external barriers that are limiting your success, and show you where you should focus your efforts to unleash your sales success. If you manage a team, think about these questions in the context of the individuals on your team, as well as yourself. Remember, this is your life, your goals, and your potential, so be honest.

Do you think you can improve sales in the next quarter? What about next year?

When answering the question above, did you think about the problems or issues that are holding you back, or the reasons for failure?

Do you doubt yourself?

Do you think others have concerns about your abilities?

Do you think other people on your team can improve their sales results? Do you believe in their success and the success of your company?

Can you excel and improve sales despite these doubts, issues and problems?

How do you plan to overcome these challenges and achieve your goals?

Can you identify and prioritize the specific areas you need to improve, in order to reach your goals? (e.g. knowledge gaps, skill shortages, poor attitudes, toxic culture, outdated sales tools, ineffective work processes)

Can you choose sales success as your reality, and work daily on specific areas that require improvement?

Can you focus on your plan without focusing on the outcome?

If you answer these questions with integrity, you should know whether you are a great supporter of your cause - your success. Keep in mind that believing in your success is a necessary first step, but without a plan and focused daily effort, you won't get there. If you need help identifying gaps and removing obstacles to your sales potential, we're here to get you on the right track.

Developing Persuasive Communication Skills

Communication is the foundation of all personal and professional relationships. It helps people express their feelings and emotions. Communication is even more important when it comes to running a business or running an organization.

Successful business leaders use communication to build a healthy relationship between their employees, customers, and business partners. Moreover, communication also plays an essential role in the success of any organization or company. Business leaders who know how to communicate effectively have a greater chance of success as individuals and entrepreneurs.

Persuasive communication is a form of communication that involves persuading or guiding listeners or readers toward adopting certain attitudes, actions, and ideas through emotional or rational means.

Many individuals involved in business use persuasive communication every day especially when making transactions. Regardless of their position, persuasive communication is important in achieving their goals and achieving success in their careers.

Persuasive communication skills are among the most important skills that business leaders, managers, and employees must possess. A good persuasive communicator has the ability to influence people to behave in a certain way. He knows how to deal with problems, eliminate conflicts and make plans. Persuasive communication skills go hand in hand with good listening skills and good management.

Being a good persuasive communicator is not an easy task. Persuasive communicators must learn how to be honest with themselves. They must know how to act and speak naturally to effectively persuade their listeners and readers. Individuals with good persuasive communication skills are able to gain the trust of others in an honest way. They don't make false claims and statements or distort the truth just to convince more people.

Effective persuasive communication requires positive relationships and trust. Individuals with good persuasive communication skills take time to understand their target audience. They try to identify their audience's goals as well as their interests. Persuasive communicators also understand the importance of listening to the opinions and objections of their target audience. By being good listeners, persuasive communicators can gain new information about the wants, interests, and concerns of their target audience.

Individuals with good persuasive communication skills can convince their target audience to try the product or services they offer. They can also convince them to promote their products and services to other people.

There are several methods that individuals can use to enhance their persuasive communication skills, such as:

• Use rational and emotional methods

The persuasive communicator must learn to understand the target market, including its interests, dislikes, and frustrations. Based on the information they have gathered, they can think of a better way to address and persuade their audience.

• Enhance your credibility and reputation

Persuasive communicators are more likely to command the respect and trust of a broader audience if they enhance their reputation for providing honest and reliable information about their intentions, goals, and ideas. Persuasive communication skills are not useful if communicators do not have the credibility that would help encourage people to listen and connect with them.

• Talk less and do more

People tend to get tired of callers who talk more, especially when the topic is not relevant anymore. In most cases, persuasive communicators don't need to talk much about their services, products, or intentions. This idea is more effective when applied to younger generations.

• Use a tactful tone

Persuasive communicators must be tactful when speaking to their target market regardless of the age and gender of their audience. In fact, they would be better off treating their target audience as mature, intelligent individuals who want to be treated as such.

• Provide conclusive evidence

A persuasive communicator needs to provide evidence that will help individuals be more willing to support their goals or sponsor their services or products. Having strong evidence will help convince individuals that any message the communicator is trying to convey will lead to positive results.

The issues addressed by persuasive communicators should reflect their communication skills, sincerity, and questioning skills. It is important that communicators take some time to practice what they will present. They should also explain what people can expect from their offerings.

If necessary, persuasive communicators should cite some examples or examples that will help individuals better understand their ideas or intentions.

Persuasive communication skills are useful for businesses. However, these skills are only used for good manners. Persuasive communication skills should never be used to deceive others for the benefit of the company or organization.

They should never be used as a tool to disparage others or make false accusations against their competitors. Success can be best experienced if it is achieved in a proper manner and through hard work and determination.

Building and Nurturing Profitable Relationships

Few would dispute the idea that building business relationships is crucial in professional services. While marketers typically focus on pricing, service strategy, and how to articulate their company's competitive positioning, the primary goal is to build trust – and ultimately relationships.

An important research study conducted by Hinge, Inside the Buyer's Brain, found that most buyers trying to choose a company rely heavily on the company's relevant experience and expertise. These factors are represented by two of the first three bars in the chart below. This goes without saying – if buyers know you're an expert in your service area, they'll be more likely to buy from you.

Like any personal relationship, business relationships require constant maintenance. Establishing mutually beneficial and communication channels are important components of success. In the long run, having close, trusted contacts will give you an advantage, especially when other marketing tactics don't work.

Here are 5 keys to building and maintaining business relationships:

1. Communicate routinely with important contacts

Frequent and personal communication with every contact in your CRM system is not only unrealistic, but rarely delivers the expected ROI. In other words, there is a time and place for widespread (but always informative and educational) email communication. However, there is a strong case to be made for routinely reaching out to contacts who closely align with the type of business you want to sell more of. Do your homework before reaching out to them. Is there an opportunity to congratulate them on the addition of their service line, a new website, or a new team member? Even if you're just reaching out to make them aware of a specific service or offering, craft your messaging in a way that's uniquely focused on them. Communicating with them first before it comes to you will enhance their experience and the overall relationship. Try to do this type of awareness regularly. If you let too much time pass, your final communication will seem less sincere.

Finally, don't ignore the power of LinkedIn. When done right, your social media strategy becomes the digital sister of in-person communication — and can be a quick and effective way to stay in touch. And try to interact with the content your contact creates or shares. It's a great way to build goodwill and establish a professional relationship.

2. Offer help before you ask for help

Building business relationships isn't about tapping into your resources when you need something. If the only time you contact a former client is when you have a new service offering, your gesture won't seem authentic. Likewise, if you only contact a seller when you're looking for a good deal, don't expect to get one.

Spend some time figuring out how you can help important contacts in your business. What value can you provide to spark the conversation?

3. Ask for feedback

Instead of assuming your customers and suppliers are happy, ask! Open communication is an essential component of any relationship.

When you ask your contacts how they feel, you promote a two-way conversation that can reveal areas for improvement. Some companies conduct customer satisfaction surveys to collect feedback. But it's usually best to pick up the phone and talk to your closest contact at the company. If this is your most important customer, you want to make sure they are satisfied.

This practice can also be an excellent business development tool. A colleague of mine once told me a story. They asked for feedback and the end of the project, and the client responded "Overall the project was great, but what I'm looking for now is XYZ. I wish your company would do that!". As it turns out, they provided this service, the customer just wasn't aware of it. A frustrating but all-too-frequent scenario in the world of professional services. Asking for feedback can go a long way toward avoiding such situations.

4. Find ways to connect with contacts in your outer circle

As new contacts enter your world, focus on building trust over time using techniques like an email newsletter. This practice helps keep your contacts informed of the latest news and resources related to your business. Since you can't personally interact with everyone in your email address book on a weekly basis, leveraging technology to do some of the work for you is a great option.

Email marketing is a powerful way to build trust and relationships. But if done incorrectly, it can easily have the opposite effect. Don't bombard your list with non targeted emails or hard offers down the funnel. Instead, focus on sending educational and informative content that your audience will find relevant and practical. There are two types of mass or automated emails that fall into this category:

"Educational emails provide content intended to provide information. These emails give something of value to the reader without asking for anything in return. Since educational emails are highly valued by your audience, they should make up about 80% of the emails you send.

Offer emails encourage the recipient to take a specific next step, such as downloading a guide or reaching out to you for a free consultation or demo. Introductory emails help move your contacts to a deeper level of engagement. Although offer emails should make up the other 20% of your overall email mix, you won't want to send them until you've first created value for your audience. Offer emails should only go to people who have already downloaded several pieces of your content. Unless they specifically ask for it, you should never email an offer to someone you just met at a networking event.

Here are some tips we've discovered for highly effective email marketing:

Make sure the look and feel of your email reflects your brand at every touchpoint.

Make sure your email template is mobile friendly.

Segment your distribution list so you can decide which emails go to which list.

Remember the 80/20 rule. No matter how much or how many emails you send, the rest (80%) should be educational, while the rest (20%) can be relevant offers.

Make sure you have a way for people to unsubscribe.

Consider the subject line carefully. To encourage high open rates, aim for 40 characters or less, and be very clear. Subject lines are not the place to be clever or leave much to the reader's imagination. Just say what the subject of the email is.

Be aware of some trigger words that can send your email straight to the recipient's spam or junk folder. Words like "cheap" or "sale," and sometimes "free," when placed in the subject line can indicate that the email is spam and will not pass the filter.

5. Educate and communicate, not tell and sell.

If building relationships requires trust and credibility, then educating on a topic relevant to your audience—rather than telling, selling, and making it all about you—is a powerful way to build professional services relationships.

The most effective way to educate your audience is to produce a steady stream of thought leadership. By definition, thought leadership marketing makes your expertise highly visible to the public. Regardless of whether your experts post on your blog, in other publications, on social media, or elsewhere, their connection to your company makes you more visible to potential clients.

The depth of content required to build your profile as a highly visible expert means potential buyers have the opportunity to learn a lot about your company before making initial contact.

This level of visibility and experience increases the trust and credibility of your company. Think of it this way: There's a reason why name brands at a grocery store sell better than store-bought brands, despite their higher price. People trust what they know."

How Will You Improve the Way You Build Business Relationships?

Building business relationships is a two-way street. Oftentimes, people in a business environment treat everything as transactional. But like relationships outside of the workplace, strong work relationships are built over time as both parties get to know, trust, and help each other.

But no two relationships are alike. This is why it is essential in the modern business environment that you use different types of technology that can help you maintain relationships. Social media platforms like LinkedIn are great for interacting with content shared by others in your network. For your part, digital newsletters and email marketing tools can help track your relationships and automate some processes.

Of course, always think about your own experience. What business relationship building techniques have worked for you?

We hope this article has stimulated some new ideas as you seek new and stronger business relationships!

Chapter 6: Leveraging Technology and Innovation

In today's rapidly evolving world, staying ahead in the competitive landscape requires a proactive approach to leveraging technology and embracing innovation. This chapter explores how you can harness the power of technology and innovation to propel your journey to $1 million in 10 months.

Harnessing the Power of Technology for Business Growth

In the fast-paced world of business, technology serves as a powerful catalyst for growth and innovation. Embracing and effectively utilizing technology can significantly enhance your organization's efficiency, productivity, and competitiveness.

1. Streamlining Operations with Digital Solutions:

Incorporating digital solutions into your business operations can streamline processes and improve overall efficiency. Implementing enterprise resource planning (ERP) software, for instance, can integrate key business functions such as finance, human resources, and supply chain management, providing real-time insights and enabling better decision-making. Additionally, cloud-based collaboration tools facilitate seamless communication and project management, allowing teams to work together effectively regardless of geographical barriers.

2. Enhancing Customer Experience through Technology:

Technology plays a pivotal role in enhancing the customer experience, leading to increased satisfaction and loyalty. Leveraging customer relationship management (CRM) systems enables businesses to track and manage interactions with customers, personalize marketing campaigns, and anticipate their needs more effectively.

Furthermore, the integration of artificial intelligence (AI) and chatbots into customer service channels can provide immediate assistance, resolve inquiries, and improve response times, thereby elevating the overall customer experience.

3. Empowering Data-Driven Decision Making:

In today's data-driven landscape, businesses have access to vast amounts of valuable information that can drive strategic decision-making. By harnessing analytics tools and technologies, organizations can gain deeper insights into market trends, customer behavior, and performance metrics. Analyzing this data empowers businesses to identify opportunities for optimization, anticipate market shifts, and tailor their strategies for maximum impact. Moreover, predictive analytics can forecast future trends and outcomes, enabling proactive decision-making and strategic planning.

4. Embracing E-Commerce and Digital Marketing:

The rise of e-commerce platforms and digital marketing channels presents unprecedented opportunities for businesses to reach and engage with their target audience. Establishing an online presence through e-commerce websites or mobile applications enables businesses to expand their reach, attract new customers, and drive sales growth. Additionally, digital marketing strategies such as search engine optimization (SEO), social media marketing, and content marketing can effectively target and engage potential customers, driving brand awareness and conversion rates.

Harnessing the power of technology is essential for driving business growth in today's digital age. By embracing digital solutions, enhancing the customer experience, leveraging data-driven insights, and embracing e-commerce and digital marketing, businesses can unlock new opportunities for innovation, efficiency, and success. Embrace technology as a strategic enabler and stay ahead of the curve in an ever-evolving business landscape.

Embracing Innovation to Stay Ahead of the Curve

Innovation is the lifeblood of successful businesses, driving growth, competitiveness, and relevance in an ever-evolving marketplace. To thrive in today's dynamic landscape, organizations must foster a culture of innovation and embrace emerging trends and technologies. This explores the importance of embracing innovation and provides insights into how businesses can stay ahead of the curve.

1. Cultivating a Culture of Creativity and Experimentation:

Innovation flourishes in environments that encourage creativity, experimentation, and risk-taking. Organizations should foster a culture that celebrates new ideas, encourages collaboration across teams, and empowers employees to challenge the status quo. By providing a supportive and inclusive workplace where employees feel empowered to innovate, businesses can unleash the full potential of their workforce and drive continuous improvement and innovation.

2. Embracing Emerging Technologies and Trends:

Innovation often stems from the adoption and integration of emerging technologies and trends into business operations. Whether it's artificial intelligence (AI), blockchain, Internet of Things (IoT), or virtual reality (VR), staying abreast of the latest technological advancements is essential for maintaining a competitive edge. By proactively exploring and experimenting with new technologies, businesses can identify opportunities for innovation, efficiency gains, and differentiation in the market.

3. Encouraging Cross-Functional Collaboration and Knowledge Sharing:

Innovation thrives when diverse perspectives and expertise come together to solve complex problems and drive change. Organizations should facilitate cross-functional collaboration and knowledge sharing initiatives to break down silos and harness the collective intelligence of their workforce. By bringing together individuals from different departments, backgrounds, and disciplines, businesses can foster creativity, spark innovation, and generate novel ideas that drive business growth and transformation.

4. Embracing a Mindset of Continuous Improvement:

Innovation is not a one-time event but a continuous process of evolution and adaptation. Businesses must adopt a mindset of continuous improvement, constantly seeking opportunities to iterate, refine, and optimize their products, services, and processes. Encouraging feedback from customers, soliciting input from employees, and monitoring industry trends are essential practices for staying agile, responsive, and innovative in a rapidly changing environment.

Embracing innovation is essential for staying ahead of the curve and driving sustained success in today's competitive business landscape. By cultivating a culture of creativity and experimentation, embracing emerging technologies and trends, fostering cross-functional collaboration, and embracing a mindset of continuous improvement, businesses can position themselves as industry leaders and innovators, poised for long-term growth and relevance. Embrace innovation as a strategic imperative and unlock new opportunities for growth, differentiation, and impact in the digital age.

Automating Processes for Efficiency and Scale

Automation has become a cornerstone of modern business operations, offering unprecedented opportunities to enhance efficiency, reduce costs, and scale operations effectively. Explores the importance of automating processes and provides insights into how businesses can leverage automation to drive efficiency and scale.

1. Identifying Opportunities for Automation:

The first step in automating processes is to identify areas within your business where automation can provide the greatest value. This may include repetitive, time-consuming tasks such as data entry, invoicing, inventory management, or customer support. By conducting a thorough assessment of your workflows and processes, you can pinpoint inefficiencies and bottlenecks that can be streamlined and automated for greater efficiency.

2. Implementing Robust Automation Solutions:

Once opportunities for automation have been identified, the next step is to implement robust automation solutions that align with your business objectives and requirements. This may involve deploying software tools, platforms, or custom-built solutions tailored to your specific needs. Whether it's workflow automation software, robotic process automation (RPA), or integrated business process management (BPM) systems, investing in the right automation technologies is essential for driving efficiency and scalability.

3. Streamlining Operations and Improving Productivity:

Automation enables businesses to streamline operations and improve productivity by eliminating manual tasks and reducing human error. By automating routine processes, employees can focus on high-value activities that require creativity, critical thinking, and problem-solving, leading to increased job satisfaction and engagement. Additionally, automation can accelerate task completion times, reduce turnaround times, and enhance overall operational efficiency, enabling businesses to achieve more with fewer resources.

4. Scaling Operations and Adapting to Growth:

As businesses grow and expand, automation becomes increasingly critical for scaling operations and maintaining competitiveness. Automated processes can easily adapt to changes in demand, volume, and complexity, allowing businesses to scale their operations efficiently without compromising quality or customer satisfaction. Whether it's scaling up production, expanding into new markets, or accommodating seasonal fluctuations, automation provides the agility and flexibility needed to support growth and expansion initiatives.

5. Monitoring Performance and Optimizing Processes:

Continuous monitoring and optimization are essential components of successful process automation initiatives. By leveraging data analytics and performance metrics, businesses can track the effectiveness of automated processes, identify areas for improvement, and optimize workflows for maximum efficiency and effectiveness. Regularly reviewing and refining automation strategies ensures that businesses remain agile, responsive, and competitive in a rapidly changing business environment.

Automating processes is essential for driving efficiency, reducing costs, and scaling operations effectively in today's competitive business landscape. By identifying opportunities for automation, implementing robust automation solutions, streamlining operations, scaling effectively, and continuously monitoring performance, businesses can unlock new levels of productivity, agility, and scalability. Embrace automation as a strategic imperative and position your business for long-term success and growth in the digital age.

Chapter 7: Building a Strong Support System

Surrounding Yourself with Positive Influences

In the pursuit of ambitious goals such as achieving $1 million in 10 months, the company you keep can significantly impact your mindset, motivation, and ultimate success. This explores the importance of surrounding yourself with positive influences and how it can propel you towards your goals.

1. Maintaining a Positive Mindset:

Surrounding yourself with positive influences begins with cultivating a positive mindset. Positive thinking can be contagious, and being around individuals who exude optimism, resilience, and enthusiasm can uplift your spirits and inspire you to stay focused on your goals, even in the face of challenges. By consciously seeking out positive thoughts and surrounding yourself with people who radiate positivity, you can create an environment that fosters growth, creativity, and success.

2. Eliminating Negative Influences:

In addition to surrounding yourself with positive influences, it's equally important to identify and eliminate negative influences from your life. Negative energy, toxic relationships, and pessimistic attitudes can drain your motivation, erode your confidence, and hinder your progress towards your goals. Take inventory of the people, environments, and activities that have a negative impact on your wellbeing, and make a conscious effort to distance yourself from them. Surround yourself with individuals who support your aspirations and believe in your potential to succeed.

3. Seeking Inspiration and Encouragement:

Surrounding yourself with positive influences also means seeking out sources of inspiration and encouragement that fuel your ambition and drive. Whether it's attending motivational events, listening to inspiring podcasts, or reading uplifting books and articles, exposing yourself to positive messages and success stories can reignite your passion and reaffirm your belief in your ability to achieve your goals. Surround yourself with content and communities that inspire you to dream big and take bold action towards realizing your aspirations.

4. Cultivating Supportive Relationships:

Building a strong support network of friends, family members, mentors, and peers who genuinely care about your success is essential for staying motivated and resilient on your journey. Surround yourself with individuals who believe in your vision, offer constructive feedback, and provide encouragement during both triumphs and setbacks. Cultivate relationships based on mutual respect, trust, and authenticity, and lean on your support system for guidance, encouragement, and accountability as you pursue your goals.

5. Being a Positive Influence Yourself:

Lastly, remember that you have the power to be a positive influence on others as well. Lead by example, embodying the qualities of optimism, resilience, and determination that you admire in others. Share your successes, setbacks, and lessons learned openly and authentically, inspiring those around you to pursue their own goals with passion and perseverance. By being a positive force in the lives of others, you not only enrich your own journey but also contribute to a culture of growth, positivity, and success within your community.

Surrounding yourself with positive influences is a powerful catalyst for achieving your goals and realizing your full potential. Cultivate a positive mindset, eliminate negative influences, seek inspiration and encouragement, cultivate supportive relationships, and be a positive influence yourself. By creating an environment that fosters optimism, resilience, and growth, you can overcome obstacles, seize opportunities, and achieve extraordinary success on your journey towards $1 million.

Chapter 8: Overcoming Challenges and Adversity

Embracing Failure as a Stepping Stone to Success

"When you fail, remember that you are only one step away from success. The setbacks you face make you smarter, more resilient, and provide you with valuable knowledge that qualifies you to achieve victory.

As I was exploring stories of success and failure in various disciplines—business, politics, academia, science, technology—I was struck by a paragraph from Forbes. "There was a man who failed in business at the age of twenty-one; He was defeated in the legislative race at the age of twenty-two; He failed again in business at the age of twenty-four; He overcame the death of his fiancée at the age of twenty-six; He had a nervous breakdown when he was 27; He lost a congressional race at age 34; Lost Senate race at age 45; He failed to become vice president at age 47; He lost the Senate race at the age of forty-nine; He was elected President of the United States at the age of 52. This man was Abraham Lincoln. He refused to let his failures define him and fought against great odds to achieve greatness" (Forbes, Five Ways to Make Peace with Failure). Further analysis of President Lincoln's efforts revealed that many doubted his skills and determination. However, he proved them all wrong.

Analyze, learn and take action

When faced with failure, treat it as a market reaction, avoiding blame, negative self-talk, and regret. Focus on learning from unsuccessful decisions whether operational, personal or non-valued market conditions. In my case, reflecting on the failures over the past 20 years, they have often been human errors. I trusted individuals who were unethical, ego-driven, and ruthless. Hence, I now prioritize starting with people, making sure that the people I choose in my life are ethical, energetic, partnership-focused, and complement my skill set. Learn to say no to anything less, because the few people you surround yourself with constitute your average. Not affected by surface; Instead, think about whether this person enhances your life and professional success.

Lesson from Adam Altman (CEO of ChatGPT)

I have carefully read and listened to articles and videos from the highly successful AI CEO Adam Altman. His relentless commitment to himself and his team stood out. He thought a lot about the possibility of failure, but he also acknowledged that the possibility of being truly right would only happen once or twice. Early in his career, Altman realized that as an ambitious person, you should "give yourself plenty of chances to get lucky." (Sam Altman, How to Be Successful).

> **Actionable Thought: Design Your Future, And Do Not Think About The Past.**

Obsessing over failure will not turn it into success. Instead, it intensifies the pain and traps you in an emotional prison with only negative choices and outcomes. Instead of dwelling on the past, focus on shaping your future. Taking positive steps toward a greater future quickly eliminates negative thoughts that are holding you back.

One of the most powerful lessons is realizing that you can know what to do in any situation, even in situations that seem impossible. The more times you do this, the more you will believe it. However, optimism is crucial. Self-confidence is the most powerful trait to achieve compound success. Successful pessimists are a rare breed."

1. Failure opens doors to new opportunities: When a startup fails, it often presents entrepreneurs with an opportunity to reflect, reevaluate their goals, and discover new ways to succeed. By embracing failure as a starting point, entrepreneurs can identify new business ideas, explore alternative markets, or point their existing ventures in a new direction.

2. Build a strong network: Failure can be a powerful communication tool. Entrepreneurs who have experienced failure firsthand often gain valuable connections and insights from their peers and mentors. By leveraging these networks, entrepreneurs can identify new opportunities, collaborate on future projects, and receive support and guidance throughout their entrepreneurial journey.

3. Utilize lessons learned for future success: Failure provides a wealth of knowledge and experience that can be applied to future endeavors. By leveraging lessons learned, entrepreneurs can make more informed decisions, avoid repeating past mistakes, and increase the chances of success in subsequent ventures.

4. Adopt a growth mindset: Failure can be a catalyst for personal and professional growth. By embracing failure as an opportunity for learning and self-improvement, entrepreneurs can develop a growth mindset that enables them to seize opportunities, adapt to change, and achieve long-term success.

A prominent example of seizing opportunities after failure is the story of Jack Ma, founder of Alibaba. Before launching Alibaba, Ma faced many failures, including a failed e-commerce project. However, he learned from these experiences and eventually founded Alibaba, which has since become one of the largest e-commerce companies in the world.

Embracing Failure As A Stepping Stone To Success
01. Failure opens door to new opportunities
02. Building a Strong network
03. Leveraging lessons learned for future success
04. Embracing a growth mindset

Developing Resilience in the Face of Obstacles

1. Flexibility in facing challenges

Facing more challenges Resilience in the face of challenges

In the dynamic landscape of entrepreneurship, resilience is emerging as a critical trait that sets successful entrepreneurs apart from the rest. It is the unwavering ability to withstand adversity, adapt to setbacks, and continue moving forward despite obstacles. In the context of "Faith and Entrepreneurship: Finding Purpose," the theme of resilience resonates deeply, intersecting with faith-driven motivations and entrepreneurial endeavors. Let's dive into the nuances of resilience, drawing insights from diverse perspectives and real-world examples:

1. Accept failure as a starting point:

- Resilient entrepreneurs realize that failure is not a dead end but a stepping stone to growth. They view setbacks as valuable learning experiences rather than insurmountable barriers.

Example: Consider the story of Jack Ma, founder of Alibaba Group. His initial venture, an online business directory, failed miserably. However, he persisted, learned from his mistakes, and eventually built one of the largest e-commerce platforms in the world.

2. Adaptive problem solving:

-Agility involves solving problems in an agile manner. Entrepreneurs who thrive under uncertainty quickly adapt to changing circumstances and find creative solutions to complex challenges.

- Example: During the COVID-19 pandemic, many small businesses faced closures. However, some restaurateurs have turned to delivery services, repurposed their spaces, or teamed up with other businesses to survive.

3. Developing mental fortitude:

Entrepreneurship can be emotionally exhausting. Resilient individuals build mental fortitude by practicing mindfulness, seeking support networks, and maintaining a positive outlook.

Example: Elon Musk, despite facing numerous setbacks with SpaceX and Tesla, maintains firm belief in his vision of sustainable energy and space exploration.

4. Rebounding from rejection:

Resilience shines when entrepreneurs face rejection, whether from investors, customers, or partners. They learn how to bounce back, improve their performances and persevere.

Example: Oprah Winfrey was fired from her first television job. Instead of giving up, she turned adversity into opportunities, eventually becoming a media mogul and philanthropist.

5. Balancing perseverance and adaptability:

- Resilience is not stubborn persistence; It's knowing when to pivot. Successful entrepreneurs recalibrate their strategies while staying true to their core purpose.

Example: Jeff Bezos started Amazon as an online bookstore. Over time, it adapted to changing market dynamics, expanding Amazon into a global e-commerce giant.

6. Drawing strength from faith:

-Faith-driven entrepreneurs find resilience in their spiritual beliefs. Whether through prayer, meditation, or community, faith provides solace during difficult times.

Example: Patricia Wertz, former CEO of Archer Daniels Midland, attributes her resilience to her Christian faith, which has guided her leadership decisions during difficult periods.

In short, flexibility is not a negative trait; It is a powerful force that drives entrepreneurs forward. As we explore the intersection between faith and entrepreneurship, let's celebrate the perseverance of those who have weathered storms, adapted, and emerged stronger on their purpose-driven journeys.

2. Flexibility in facing challenges

Obstacles and failure are inevitable in life. Everyone has faced it at one point or another, but what sets successful people apart is their ability to recover and overcome it. Resilience is the key to success, and it is a skill that can be developed and nurtured over time. In this section, we will explore the importance of resilience in the face of challenges, and how to develop it to unleash your inner hero.

1. Acknowledging and accepting failure: The first step to overcoming obstacles and failure is to acknowledge and accept them. Failure is a natural part of life, and it is important to understand that it is not the end of the world. Instead of dwelling on your mistakes, use them as learning opportunities. Analyze what went wrong, and figure out how you can do better next time. Accepting failure as part of the process will help you build resilience and bounce back stronger.

2. Develop a growth mindset: A growth mindset is the belief that your abilities and intelligence can be developed over time through hard work and dedication. This mindset allows you to view failure as a temporary setback, rather than a reflection of your abilities. It helps you stay motivated and focused on your goals, even when you face obstacles. Develop a growth mindset by embracing challenges, seeking feedback, and learning from your mistakes.

3. Set realistic goals: Setting realistic goals is essential for building resilience. When you set unrealistic goals, you set yourself up for failure. This can be frustrating and disheartening, making it difficult to recover when things don't go as planned. Instead, set achievable goals that challenge you, but are within your reach. This will help you build confidence and resilience and increase your chances of success.

4. Develop a support system: Having a strong support system can make a big difference when facing challenges and failure. Surround yourself with people who believe in you and encourage you to keep going. Look for mentors and role models who can provide guidance and support. Having a support system can help you stay motivated, stay focused on your goals, and recover from setbacks.

5. Practice self-care: Taking care of yourself is crucial to building resilience. Make sure you get enough sleep, eat a healthy diet, and exercise regularly. Practice mindfulness and meditation to reduce stress and increase mental clarity. Self-care helps you stay focused and centered, even when facing challenges.

Building resilience is essential to overcoming obstacles and failure. By acknowledging and accepting failure, developing a growth mindset, setting realistic goals, developing a support system, and practicing self-care, you can develop the resilience needed to unleash your inner champion. Remember that resilience is a skill that can be developed and nurtured over time. With practice, you can become more resilient and achieve your goals, no matter what challenges you may face.

Turning Setbacks into Opportunities for Growth

Embracing failure as a catalyst for growth

Failure is often viewed as a negative outcome, something to be avoided at all costs. However, what if I told you that failure can actually be a stepping stone toward personal and professional growth? It may seem counterintuitive, but learning from failure is an essential part of becoming more adaptable in life. Instead of seeing setbacks as roadblocks, we can choose to see them as opportunities to grow and learn.

2. Learn from mistakes

One of the most important lessons we can learn from failure is the ability to recognize our mistakes and learn from them. When we make a mistake or face a setback, it's important to take a step back and think about what went wrong. By analyzing the situation, we can identify the factors that contributed to the failure and develop strategies to avoid making the same mistakes in the future.

For example, let's say you started a new business but it ultimately failed. Instead of dwelling on failure, take the time to evaluate what went wrong. Was it a lack of market research, poor financial planning, or ineffective marketing strategies? By identifying the root causes of failure, you can make necessary adjustments and approach future endeavors with more knowledge and insight.

3. Build resilience and perseverance

Failure can be a test of our resilience and perseverance. When you face setbacks, it's easy to get discouraged and give up. However, the ability to recover from failure is an essential characteristic of adaptability. Embracing failure as a learning opportunity allows us to develop a resilience mindset, enabling us to overcome obstacles and persevere in the face of adversity.

Take the example of J.K. Rowling, author of the hugely popular Harry Potter series. Before achieving success, Rowling faced many rejections from publishers. Instead of letting these setbacks deter her, she used them as motivation to improve her writing and seek new opportunities. Her resilience and determination eventually paid off, creating one of the most successful book franchises in history.

4. Develop a growth mindset

A growth mindset is the belief that our abilities and intelligence can be developed through dedication and hard work. Failure provides an excellent opportunity to develop this mindset. Instead of viewing failure as a reflection of our abilities, we can choose to see it as a temporary setback that can be overcome with effort and learning.

When you experience failure, it is important to adopt a growth mindset and focus on lessons learned rather than on negative outcomes. This shift in mindset allows us to approach future challenges with a sense of optimism and determination.

A real-life example of this is the story of Thomas Edison and his invention of the light bulb. Edison famously said: "I haven't failed, I've just found 10,000 ways that won't work." Despite facing many failures and setbacks, Edison continued to persist, ultimately creating one of the most influential inventions in history.

5. Seek feedback and learning opportunities

Failure provides an opportunity to get feedback and learn from others. When we face setbacks, it's essential to reach out for support and guidance. Getting feedback from mentors, peers, or experts in the field can provide valuable insights and perspectives that can help us grow and improve.

In addition, failure can be an incentive to seek new educational opportunities. Whether it's attending workshops, taking courses, or reading books on the subject, actively pursuing knowledge in areas where we've seen failure can help us develop new skills and approaches.

Failure is not the end of the road, but rather a starting point towards personal and professional growth. By embracing failure, learning from our mistakes, and cultivating a growth mindset, we can turn setbacks into opportunities for growth. Remember, resilience is not about avoiding failure, it is about bouncing back stronger and more resilient than ever before.

Chapter 9: SCALING YOUR SUCCESS

Scaling Your Business for Sustainable Growth

Entrepreneurship is a journey of constant evolution, and few challenges are as critical and complex as scaling your business. Sustainable growth is an art that requires a delicate balance between ambition and practicality, innovation and consistency. For those looking to grow their ventures responsibly, this comprehensive guide reveals expert strategies that assure lasting success.

introduction
Understanding how to scale your business effectively means realizing that growth must be progressive and sustainable. While expansion presents new opportunities for success, it also presents a set of challenges that require careful navigation to ensure longevity in the market.

Understand the fundamental pillars of sustainable expansion
Vision:
Your guiding star in the expansion process is a clear and compelling vision. It is the foundation upon which your strategies are built and is a constant reminder of where you are headed. A strong vision should be a rallying cry for your team and the promise you make to your customers.

Valuable site:
Your value proposition is the heartbeat of your company, demonstrating the unique benefits and solutions you offer. As you expand your value proposition, reevaluate and refine it to ensure it aligns with the evolving market and customer needs.

Scalability of your business model

Sustainability starts with a resilient business model; One that can withstand market shifts and expand in proportion to demand. Strategies for crafting a scalable model often include standardization, automation, and flexible workforce arrangements, allowing for growth without over-expansion.

Case studies like Patagonia highlight a commitment to sustainable practices as an integral part of their expansion. Likewise, Airbnb's sharing economy model demonstrates the power of innovative approaches to scalability.

Building a strong organizational culture

Company culture is the soil from which all growth emerges. To scale sustainably, foster a culture characterized by shared values, open communication, and mutual respect. Hiring individuals who not only have the required skills, but also fit organically into your culture is crucial. Investing in your team's professional and personal growth will also contribute to long-term success.

Implementing effective systems and processes

Efficiency and consistency are vital as your business grows. This includes creating robust systems and processes, technology integration, and a commitment to continuous improvement.

"Sustainable expansion is not just about growth; It's about conscious expansion that respects the environment and nurtures the community.

Developing strategic partnerships

Strategic collaboration can provide the leverage needed for scalable growth. Through partnerships, companies can share resources, knowledge and networks. For example, Warby Parker attributes part of its success to strategic partnerships that align with its ethos and contribute to sustainable expansion.

Measure and monitor progress

What gets measured gets managed. To scale sustainably, it is essential to track progress using key performance indicators (KPIs). This allows rapid responses to market fluctuations and ensures growth objectives are aligned with overall strategic objectives.

Conclusion

Through these strategies, entrepreneurs can navigate the complexities of expansion with confidence and insight. The goal is not just to expand, but to grow thoughtfully and intentionally, creating businesses that last and thrive in a dynamic economic landscape.

Remember the words of John Smith, "The key to lasting success is the ability to scale without losing sight of your core values and the unique spark that ignited your business."

Quick takeaways for entrepreneurs:

- Regularly revisit your vision and value proposition.
- Building a flexible and scalable business model.
- Promoting an organizational culture that supports sustainable growth.
- Implement systems and processes that streamline operations.
- Develop strategic partnerships that advance your business goals.
- Keep a close eye on key metrics to guide your growth journey.

By embedding these principles into the core of your business, you prepare not only for growth, but for sustainable success that resonates with your customers, empowers your employees, and benefits the broader community. Let these expert strategies guide your path as you rise to unprecedented levels, inspiring a future where entrepreneurial success and sustainability go hand in hand.

Expanding Your Reach and Impact

Let's face it. Expanding your business is difficult. It takes a lot of effort. At first, this means wearing different hats. It means dealing with sales and marketing. This means understanding taxes and corporate compliance. It involves having to interact with customers on a daily basis. And much more. At the end of the day, it takes a toll on you.

If you're struggling to grow your business, there is a light at the end of the tunnel. Sure, it's difficult. But, what is the alternative? Life sucks 9 to 5 jobs? Of course not. Well, maybe you crave a guaranteed salary. But at what mental or emotional cost will that come?

the truth? If you do your best, clear your mind, and look at things in perspective, you can easily identify ways in which you can grow your business and make more money quickly. While there are likely hundreds of business growth strategies, the following 15 will take your business to the next level quickly and efficiently.

Roland Fraser, a business growth strategist, has a unique approach to scaling a business. As a Master Digital Marketer, Native Commerce Media, and CEO of War Room Mastermind, he knows a thing or two about the world of online marketing.

Fraser, who builds and scales seven-, eight- and nine-figure businesses, tells me there are a lot of ways to grow a business quickly. But, there are only 15 essential strategies that will have a real impact on your bottom line. Some of them take a long time at first. This should be expected often. But the benefits and profits will eventually make it worthwhile.

Like anything else in life or business, you have to make time if you are looking to reap the benefits. Don't focus on the short-term results of your work. Look at the long term.

Build honest value and look to help your customers. Real care. This should be the basis. After that, it's simply a matter of taking action and doing the work at scale.

1. Build a sales funnel.

The number one way to grow your business quickly is to build a sales funnel. If you don't have a sales funnel, you're making a huge mistake. Sales funnels can help automate your business. It helps you expand and grow quickly and easily. Sure, there's some front-end work involved. clearly. But once these processes are in place, it's smooth sailing from there.

Fraser says that every sales funnel should be carefully conceptualized before it is created. Think about the different conversion paths first and foremost. Whether it's a free plus shipping offer or a high-cost training course, it's important to create your own automated vending machine to scale and grow your business quickly.

2. Utilize the customer management system.

It is difficult to track transactions manually. Nobody wants to do that. It becomes very stressful as the business grows. If you want to scale quickly, use a customer management system. There are so many to choose from. But it really depends on your industry. Of course, cloud software like SalesForce is always a viable option.

Quickbooks can help you with accounting. InfusionSoft can also help with sales and marketing. There are a lot of content management systems (CMS), most of which integrate with other cloud services. Find what works for you and use it.

3. Look for competition.

When you go to market, and are really looking to get your offering out to the masses, you need to look out for the competition. Fraser says he uses two platforms to conduct his research. The first is a similar network. The other, AdBeat. Both provide competitive information. It's your chance to get X-ray lenses into all landing pages, ad copy and other stages of the conversion funnel.

This allows you to uncover the strategy of any online advertiser. Find ads that have been running longer and emulate them. This is the fastest way to scale any business. If it works for your competitors, it will likely work for you.

4. Create a customer loyalty program.
Loyalty programs are great ways to increase sales. It costs up to three times as much to acquire new customers as it does to sell something to an existing customer. Other resources peg this number anywhere from four to 10 times more. However, any way you slice it, acquiring new customers is expensive.

Building a customer loyalty program will help you retain customers, Fraser says. It may also help you attract new people as well. If there is a clear incentive to spend more money with you, it will pay off in the long run. Create an attractive loyalty program, make it accessible to your existing customers, and watch sales skyrocket over time.

5. Identify new opportunities.
Analyze new opportunities in your business by better understanding your demographics. Understand everything from distribution channels to your direct competitors, to analysis of foreign markets and other potential industries. There are likely dozens of new opportunities that you can immediately pursue with the right amount of analysis.

"6. Build an email list. One of the best and most effective ways to grow a business quickly is to build an email list. Obviously, this means you need a lead magnet. Why would people subscribe to your list? And with a lead magnet comes the need for a sales funnel. Look for companies like Aweber, ConstantContact, ConvertKit, Drip, GetResponse, and others to build and manage your list.

7. Forming strategic partnerships. Strategic partnerships with the right companies can make a big difference. It can allow you to reach a wide range of customers quickly. Identifying those partnerships may be easier said than done. But look for companies that complement yours. Contact them and suggest opportunities to work together.

8. Take advantage of global platforms. In the field of e-commerce selling products? Why not use Amazon's FBA service? In the field of selling services? Why not use Upwork? In the vacation home rental business? Why not take advantage of AirBnB, InvitedHome, HomeAway or other global platforms? Find a platform that has reached saturation and use it to grow your business quickly.

9. Licensing Deals Doing licensing deals is a great way to grow your business without a lot of extra effort. If you have a product that you can license to others and share the revenue, this is an ideal way to grow quickly. Taking a popular or successful product and bringing it to a company with a large footprint can help you achieve market saturation faster.

10. Consider the franchise model. If you have a successful business and are really looking to grow quickly, consider franchising it. Although franchise costs are high and transitioning to a franchise model is complex and requires a lot of marketing knowledge, it can make a big difference if you are really looking for rapid growth.

11. Diversify your offerings. Consider diversifying your offerings. What complementary products, services or information can you offer in your business? In order to grow, you have to think about expansion. Identify new opportunities in your field of specialization. Detecting pain points. What can you sell to your customers? Where else can you add value on the stock market?

12. Build passive income sources. Growing a business takes a lot of effort. If you're dealing with razor-thin profit margins, consider creating passive income streams. This way, you don't have to worry as much about keeping the lights on, so to speak. Passive income will provide you with the opportunity to make mistakes and you will not have to lose your shirt. This will keep you in business and provide a foundation to grow, market and expand quickly by giving you adequate resources.

13. Acquisition of other businesses. Sometimes, acquiring other businesses is a very quick way to grow your own business. If you can find competitors or companies in other industries that will complement yours, you can use them as platforms to expand quickly. Take a look inside your industry and even outside it to find the potential for potential opportunities.

14. International expansion. Can you expand internationally? Can you take your existing offerings and expand them internationally? What does it take to do business in Canada, Mexico or Europe? If you have a transforming proposition, international expansion can be a quick way to grow. You will incur some costs. certainly. But the potential for profits can be huge.

15. Create a webinar. Webinars are a great way to promote any product or service. It can also help you grow any business relatively quickly. Webinars provide an automated selling tool to take literally any product or service to market and reach a wide audience quickly. A webinar broker is great for engaging audiences to get the after sale automatically."

Leaving a Lasting Legacy of Success

After the first part of a recent workshop, a senior leader approached me and made this confession: "Based on what I learned today, I've been a terrible leader for ten years. I've wasted a lot of time leading from a transactional standpoint. Checking boxes on a to-do list My own business and moving things forward I never thought I could impact the business through true appreciation for the individual - including myself as an individual!

I was not shocked by what he said. When people like me do our work, it forces leaders to confront their mindsets around our topics. In my case, we were talking about individuality and influence. But confronting the mentality is one thing and changing it is another. We've all fallen victim to the 'Monday morning effect' of workshops – where we're so dazzled by the possibilities that we forget when the daily grind returns. Will this person be a victim? Did he sense—not just understand—the importance of what he was saying? It made him think a little more.

"If you retired today, what legacy would you leave behind?"

He thought for a moment and then said, "It's disappointing, because I've been so focused on what I'm responsible for and so insensitive to who I'm responsible for as a leader."

What then did this commander tell me about what he was responsible for? Deal. He had an executive mindset centered around success alone, not a legacy mindset centered around importance.

Legacy is about reinventing growth, and this leader, like all the leaders in the room – and by extension their companies – has forgotten how leadership plays a role in making sure what we do goes beyond the next sale or deal. Inheritance is not determined by how much you sell. This may define your success but legacy is about importance and goes beyond the bottom line. Legacy is also not measured by how much you undo the legacy of those who came before you, as is the current state of our political affairs with repeated efforts to roll back the Affordable Care Act.

Legacy is how you impact others in the workplace, marketplace, and community over the long term.

Leaders must think of their legacy as something more holistic, something that impacts beyond selfish gains and which side you're on. But like the leader I spoke to, they often don't. Instead, leaders think linearly about the deal, and many will come away with the same sense of disappointment: that their legacy doesn't even matter to them.

But what do we expect when we spend more time judging the people around us instead of finding and understanding the value that lies within each individual that can help us make better decisions? Can we help people rise to become more than just what their job title says they are? This is what helps build brands that last a lifetime. Remember, Sam Walton not only wanted to shake the doorman's hand at every store he visited, but the doorman wanted to shake his hand, too. (A story that remains relevant as captured by a recent New York Times story about the paths of two janitors from two different companies a generation apart.)

Simply put, we don't talk about legacy enough — we don't have legacy mindsets. We focus on advancing our own agendas. Instead of listening to others and seeing them as individuals, we try to control them. But what everyone is learning is that employees and consumers have much more influence over organizations and their leaders than they think. If they fail to meet the unique needs and differences of individuals, they will fail to unleash individual potential and associated outcomes as the ultimate foundation for building legacy.

Simply put, the importance comes more to those who are surrounded by people who want their success to continue. People who build their success as an individual by stripping others of their individuality will never create significance. People who define their success as simply being more successful than their parents, the previous generation, their friends and neighbors, or the competition are climbing a ladder that leads to more "stuff" and selfishness, not importance to others.

Yes, if you are a billionaire, you can end your life generously to try to get over the way you treated others in the past. I always come back to the story of Andrew Carnegie, who used his success in railroads and other businesses to become one of the greatest philanthropists of all time. Many important things have come from this philanthropy, from Carnegie Mellon University to libraries. Unfortunately, Carnegie built his success as a brutal president who was notorious for abusing his people. Is this the legacy you want? Most of us don't have the billions to build a new legacy. The best thing we can do is change our mindset now and ask: What is my purpose? Why am I here? Only then will we change our mindsets authentically and personally.

Success is great, but the way we measure it often fails to take into account its importance to others and to ourselves. Professor Robert M. And UC San Francisco bought into this idea in a New York Times op-ed titled "How Measurement is Failing Us": "Our practical efforts to measure and improve quality are now hindering the altruism, and even love, that motivates people to enter the helping professions. As we search for how to improve, we need to Moving more lightly in evaluating the work of professionals who practice in our most humane and sacred fields Wachter was talking about doctors and lawyers, but we can't limit that to health care and law, because we're all human — or at least we need to be a little more so.

Conclusion

As we reach the end of 10 Months to $1 Million: Unlocking the Path to Financial Freedom, it's important to reflect on the transformative journey we've been on together. This book was more than just a collection of strategies and tips; It was a comprehensive blueprint for reshaping your mindset, redefining your approach to wealth, and achieving exceptional financial success in a remarkably short period.

The principles and ideas shared in these pages are not theoretical musings but practical, actionable steps drawn from real-world experiences and proven methodologies. The journey to $1 million in ten months is an undeniably ambitious one, but as I've learned, it's entirely achievable with the right mindset, strategic planning, and consistent execution.

Embrace the power of your mindset

One of the most profound lessons in this book is the tremendous power of your mindset. The way you think about money, success, and your own potential can move you toward your goals or hold you back. By adopting a millionaire mindset, you unleash the ability to see opportunities where others see obstacles, to persist where others give up, and to innovate where others stagnate. Remember that your thoughts shape your reality, and develop a mindset that aligns with your highest aspirations.

Implement strategic goal setting and action planning

The journey to financial freedom is made with clear vision and strategic planning. You've learned how to set SMART goals, create a detailed action plan, and break down your goals into manageable steps. As you move forward, continue to refine your goals, monitor your progress, and adjust your strategies as needed. Stay focused, stay disciplined, and keep your eye on the prize.

Taking advantage of technology and innovation

In a world where technology is evolving at an amazing pace, your ability to take advantage of the latest developments will be a critical factor in your success. Whether it's through automating processes, using data analytics, or embracing digital marketing, let technology be a catalyst for efficiency and growth on your journey. Innovation is not just about adopting new tools, it is also about fostering a culture of creativity and continuous improvement within yourself and your organization.

Build and maintain a strong support system

Success is rarely achieved in isolation. Surround yourself with positive influences, seek guidance from those who have walked the path before you, and build a network of supportive peers. Your journey will undoubtedly have ups and downs, and having a strong support system can provide the encouragement, guidance, and accountability needed to persevere and thrive. And remember, together we are stronger.

Commitment to continuous learning and adaptation

The path to a million dollars is dynamic and ever-changing. Commitment to lifelong learning, remaining adaptable, and remaining open to new ideas and perspectives. By constantly seeking knowledge and embracing change, you put yourself in a position to capitalize on emerging opportunities and overcome challenges with agility and confidence.

As you close this book, know that you are equipped with the knowledge, tools, and mindset needed to achieve financial freedom and beyond. The journey you embark on is not just about accumulating wealth, it is about creating a life of purpose, impact, and fulfillment. Every step you take, every goal you achieve, and every challenge you overcome brings you closer to achieving your true potential.

"From 10 Months to a Million Dollars" is your guide, guide, and companion on this transformational journey. Embrace your inner principles, take bold action, and believe in your ability to achieve extraordinary success. Your path to financial freedom is ahead of you – launch it with determination, resilience, and unwavering belief in your vision. The journey starts now."

www.ingramcontent.com/pod-product-compliance
Lightning Source LLC
Chambersburg PA
CBHW082209220526
45470CB00010B/3099